YO-AQU-277

Religion
in Tennessee
1777–1945

Religion in Tennessee 1777–1945

BY HERMAN A. NORTON

PUBLISHED IN COOPERATION WITH

The Tennessee Historical Commission

THE UNIVERSITY OF TENNESSEE PRESS

KNOXVILLE

TENNESSEE THREE STAR BOOKS / *Paul H. Bergeron, General Editor*

This series of general-interest books about significant Tennessee topics is sponsored jointly by the Tennessee Historical Commission and the University of Tennessee Press. Inquiries about manuscripts should be addressed to Professor Bergeron, History Department, University of Tennessee, Knoxville. Orders and questions concerning titles in the series should be addressed to the University of Tennessee Press, Knoxville, 37916.

Copyright © 1981 by The University of Tennessee Press / Knoxville.
All rights reserved.
Manufactured in the United States of America.
First edition.

Clothbound editions of University of Tennessee Press books are printed on paper designed for an effective life of at least 300 years, and binding materials are chosen for strength and durability.

Library of Congress Cataloging in Publication Data

Norton, Herman Albert.
  Religion in Tennessee, 1777–1945.

  (Tennessee three star books)
  Bibliography: p.
  Includes index.
  1. Tennessee—Church history. I. Title. II. Series.
BR555.T2N67   280'.09768   81-1562
ISBN 0-87049-317-5
ISBN 0-87049-318-3 (pbk.)

ABOUT THE AUTHOR:

Herman A. Norton is Dean of the Disciples Divinity House and Professor of Church History at Vanderbilt University.

Cover Photograph: Church in Cades Cove. Photograph copyright © 1981 by Bill Deane.

To Alma, Virginia, and Steve

Preface

Religion has always been an important ingredient in Tennessee life. From the time the first settlers moved into the valleys of the Holston and Watauga rivers to the present-day, religious organizations have had a major social and cultural role in the growth of the state. As the population grew so did denominations and the enterprises they sponsored. But the movement from a few scattered Protestant gatherings, containing less than a thousand members, to Protestant, Roman Catholic, and Jewish congregations embracing over one and a half million adherents, however, while steady, has been very uneven. This volume recounts the broad development of organized religion in Tennessee from 1777, the date of the first resident minister in the state, to 1945 in the mid-twentieth century, the logical stopping point because of the "new age" created by the atomic explosions in August 1945 and by the end of World War II.

This narrative constitutes a general history of organized religion in Tennessee. Restrictions on space preclude detailed accounts of denominations or biographies of ministers within the state. A few denominations, however, received what may seem to some disproportionate attention; when this occurs, it is because of the strategic role of those particular organizations in the life of Tennesseans. Similarly, there are recitals of the accomplishments of some ministers; I hope that these sketches of a few preachers will provide a representative cross-section of the many who have labored diligently and well. But in the main, this volume emphasizes broad general themes that identify the major contributions to the heritage in which present-day Tennesseans share. Although this story is related chronologically, it crystalizes around important issues and events.

I have made a determined effort to be objective, to render a balanced, impartial, and accurate composition of good and bad, pleasant and unpleasant, achievements and failures. On controversial issues especially, impartiality has been my guiding standard.

No book is ever the product of an individual. Directly and indirectly, many contribute to a published work. Consequently, a debt of everlasting gratitude is due those who wrote articles, pamphlets, and local church histories, as well as those who kept diaries. The editors of various religious periodicals provided immeasurable background aid when they wrote editorials and news items. The bibliography acknowledges the published volumes that proved especially helpful. All of these, along with friends and colleagues who have made helpful suggestions, have made this a more reliable volume.

Vanderbilt University   HERMAN NORTON
November 1980

Contents

ILLUSTRATIONS

Religion
in Tennessee
1777–1945

1. Seed Time

Samuel Doak was disturbed. Little wonder! He had just become aware that he was the first and only resident minister in the territory that was to become Tennessee. Even the colorful foliage, bathed in the warm sun of October 1777, failed to alter his mood. Licensed by Hanover Presbytery in Virginia six months earlier, Doak had ridden into the backwoods expecting the companionship of at least a few colleagues. Although some ministers had traveled in and out of the area, none had established residency. And church members were almost as scarce as clergymen.

The Scotch-Irish had been among the earliest settlers in Tennessee, and with them had come Presbyterianism. A strong and determined people twice expatriated, first from Scotland and later from Ireland, they found America the land of hope. Soon after arriving on the eastern shore of Maryland and the Carolinas, major ports of entry, they moved through the seaboard region to possess the frontiers of Virginia and the Carolinas. It was not long before they, in company with other Scottish immigrants in quest of some good land, began moving into the Watauga and Holston river valleys of eastern Tennessee.

Living by wit, rifle, and brain in a crude life full of danger, these strong-willed, well-muscled, courageous people established small Presbyterian congregations almost as steadily as they constructed shelters, cleared the fields, and wrested a living from the land. Through these congregations, the Presbyterians gave a religious tone to the settlements, and efforts were made to secure ministers to place religion on a firmer basis and exert a strong moral influence in the communities. But there were too few of the Scotch-Irish clergy who wanted to redeem the people of the West. Doak, however, moved by a missionary zeal, had sought the frontier. At the time of his arrival, the area had passed from uninhabited wilderness to the Watauga settlement. He was actively at work as it successively became the Watauga Association, the State of

Franklin, the Southwest Territory, and eventually, in 1796, part of the State of Tennessee.

Doak's arrival had been preceded by the appearance of the Reverend Charles Cummings, who is generally believed to have been the first Presbyterian minister to visit Tennessee. A resident of Abingdon, Virginia, Cummings began to serve two congregations along the banks of the Holston River as early as 1772, only three years after the first settlement by William Bean in the Tennessee territory. On these trips he was, of necessity, an example of precaution. Sunday morning he would "put on his shot-pouch, shoulder his rifle, mount his stallion, and ride off to church." When he met his congregation, each man had a rifle in his hand. Laying aside his rifle, Cummings "would preach two sermons, with a short interval between." As he traveled through the area, he preached some of the first discourses ever heard in the forts and settlements, and he kindled the desire for greater ministerial activity.

In response to that desire, Doak came into Tennessee territory. He arrived with impressive credentials. A program of classical study in the school that eventually became Washington and Lee University had been followed by two years at Princeton and the award of a baccalaureate degree in 1775. Teaching two years as a member of the faculty at Hampden-Sydney College, Doak had simultaneously studied theology under the guidance of the college president, the Reverend John Blair Smith. He also had a ministerial apprenticeship before receiving his license at age twenty-eight from the Hanover Presbytery, which extended its boundaries to the East Tennessee region.

Doak settled and preached initially in what is now Sullivan County. Stationing himself between the forks of the Holston and Watauga rivers, he spent two years moving among the settlers providing religious leadership. In 1780, he moved to the Salem settlement in present-day Washington County. He decided on the relocation, according to tradition, after an impressive experience with some settlers who were cutting trees. He had been riding through the forest when he met the men. Learning his identity, they requested he delay his journey and preach to as many people as could be assembled immediately. With the grove as a sanctuary and his horse as a pulpit, he delivered a sermon. Deeply moved, the settlers begged him to come and live among them. Doak and his small family soon became Salem residents. Once settled, the young

Samuel Doak, Tennessee's first resident minister and educator.

minister led in the erection of a log structure to house the congregation, the first Presbyterian church building in Tennessee.

The energetic Doak was not only a good pastor but an aggressive evangelist as well. In the same year that the congregation at Salem was constituted, he established gatherings at New Providence, Carter's Valley, and Mount Bethel. Additionally, he had a hand in organizing worshipers at Upper Concord, New Bethel, and Hebron, all in East Tennessee. A contemporary was correct in his assessment: "[This] stern, hard, God-fearing man became a most powerful influence for good throughout the whole formative period."

But Doak was not content to spend his energies solely in the arena of religion, for he immediately became involved in academic endeavors. Doak, Tennessee's first resident minister, was also the region's first and most prominent academician. No sooner was the building completed to house the Salem congregation than a second structure was under construction to accommodate a school. In 1783, Martin Academy, named in honor of the governor of North Carolina, Josiah Martin, was founded. It was the first educational institution between the Alleghenies and the Mississippi River. In 1795, a charter for Washington College, named in honor of the nation's first President, was secured. Still later, Doak assisted his second son in founding Tusculum Academy, later to become Tusculum College. These institutions played a vital role in bringing culture to the frontier. Equally significant, graduates of Doak's schools, including his two sons, John and Samuel, took the lead in establishing Presbyterian congregations and schools. But it was Gideon Blackburn, an honor graduate, who set the pace.

Combining the fire and energy of his teacher with a spirit of kindness and sympathy foreign to most pioneer preachers, Blackburn became one of the best-known ministers on the frontier. He began his ministerial activity in 1792, at the age of twenty, as pastor of the New Providence and Eusebia congregations in the Maryville area. Soon he was preaching at several different forts and communities where congregations were later organized. He preached among the Cherokees and was instrumental in taking Presbyterianism across the Cumberland Mountains to the area around Nashville.

Blackburn possessed a commanding physical appearance and an un-

---

Gideon Blackburn, who led in the establishment of Presbyterianism in the areas around Knoxville and Nashville.

usually eloquent and persuasive preaching ability. He usually attracted an appreciative audience wherever he gave a discourse. His sermons, widely discussed by those who heard them, were often prepared as he worked at manual labor. For example, while he ploughed, Blackburn would often have a piece of paper and an inkhorn on a stump at the end of the field. When he came to the end of a row, he would record on the paper the main headings of a sermon. While continuing to work, he would review the skeleton speech, periodically stopping to write down the ideas that had come to him, until he had filled out each major part. Many a discourse that reeked of fire and brimstone was prepared as he tilled the soil.

Other clergymen came to the aid of Doak and the graduates of his educational institutions in spreading Presbyterianism up and down the East Tennessee valleys and across the plateau to the Cumberland area. Hezekiah Balch moved into the region from North Carolina; Samuel Carrick and Isaac Anderson came from Virginia.

Balch, a Princeton classmate of Doak's, came to the area to take charge of the Mount Bethel congregation that Doak had organized. The church prospered under his ministry. In 1794 he obtained a charter for Greeneville College, which, some seventy-five years later, merged with neighboring Tusculum College. Balch, however, "overbearing and abusive in his views," was also responsible for the denomination losing ground when he accepted a doctrine known as Hopkinsianism—a minute departure from strict Calvinism. Balch's action caused intense controversy and led several ministers to withdraw and form an independent presbytery. This was Tennessee's first religious controversy.

Carrick led in the organization of a congregation at present-day Knoxville and then founded a school that evolved into Blount College, East Tennessee University, and later the University of Tennessee. Meanwhile, Anderson preached extensively in private homes and outdoors throughout the area around Knoxville and eventually led in the establishment of Maryville College.

After first securing a foothold in East Tennessee, Presbyterianism had spread as far west as the Nashville area by 1785, the year the Abingdon Presbytery was established, and the congregations in Tennessee were placed under its jurisdiction. Thomas Craighead, another graduate of Princeton, arrived at Nashville on a Saturday afternoon early in 1785. The following day he mounted a stump and preached the first Presbyterian sermon ever heard in the area. During the year, Craighead established residency about six miles from Nashville at Haysboro, a village no longer existing and marked today only by Spring Hill Cemetery, where a small stone building was constructed for use as a church and school. Meanwhile, William McGee was at Shiloh, near Gallatin, preaching and teaching.

By the time Tennessee became the sixteenth state in 1796, the foundation for Presbyterianism had been firmly established. With twenty-seven congregations stretching from East Tennessee to the Nashville area, of which the vast majority were in the east, John Calvin's spiritual descendants had become the state's most powerful religious force. And Presbyterians in those early days were associated so closely with education that they virtually monopolized it.

The success that attended Presbyterianism had been due primarily to the caliber of the ministry and the Scotch-Irish constituency. The ministers, with their varied talents, untiring zeal, and thorough consecration, had brought honor to their calling. Detesting the British more than Satan, the Scotch-Irish of the region gave unwavering support to the colonies in their struggle for independence. The activity coincided with the effort of the Presbyterians to become established and won respect and appreciation for the denomination. Samuel Doak dramatized the activity of the Scotch-Irish, clergy and lay alike, when he met a company of about 100 riflemen from the Watauga and Holston communities in late September 1780, prior to the decisive battle which followed at King's Mountain on October 7. Tradition claims he offered a prayer and then, after admonishing the soldiers to be courageous, said: "Go forth, and may the sword of the Lord and of Gideon go with you."

On the scene in Tennessee, simultaneously with the Presbyterians, were the Baptists. Enticed by fertile lands and diminishing danger, settlers of the Baptist persuasion, both lay and clerical, moved across the Alleghenies into the territory from homes in Virginia and North Carolina. Theologically, they were primarily of two types. The Regular Baptists, strict Calvinists of English origin and initially called Particular Baptists, were the more numerous. The Separate Baptists, modified Calvinists who had withdrawn from established New England denominations during the Great Awakening prior to the American Revolution, had a smaller constituency. In 1787 the majority in each group merged to form the United Baptists, a term used at least a decade earlier in Tennessee.

Early Baptist congregations organized for the most part before there were pastors to serve them. Founding a Baptist congregation was simple; no ecclesiastical hierarchy had to be consulted. Organization came when a little band, who had discovered a fellowship, desired to form a congregation. Baptists were fitted for the frontier.

The initial permanent Baptist congregation was very likely the one at Sinking Creek, organized in 1775 in present-day Carter County, following a revival in the home of Charles Robertson. Indisputably, the second church formed by the Baptists was in 1779 at Buffalo Ridge on Boone's Creek, eight miles north of present-day Jonesboro, by a group which moved from a congregation at Sandy Creek, North Carolina. This conformed to a pattern. Baptists often would come in a body from Virginia and North Carolina congregations and constitute the nucleus for a Tennessee church. At least five Baptist congregations came into existence this way in 1781 alone. By 1786, the Baptists had sufficient strength to establish the Holston Association, the first such organization west of the Allegheny Mountains.

At the time the Holston Association was being formed, Baptists were also arriving and organizing the area "watered by the Cumberland River." In 1786, a congregation was constituted in present-day Montgomery County by Joseph Grammer at Sulphur Fork, a branch of the Red River. Indian hostility forced a dissolution of the congregation, but in 1791 another church was successfully established at the same site. Three years later at White's Creek, about six miles north of Nashville, the first Baptist church was formed in present-day Davidson County. In 1795 a second church appeared at Sulphur Fork when a congregation, formed in North Carolina, migrated as a group to the area immediately after organizing, accompanied by their pastor, Joseph Davis. Thus when Tennessee was admitted to statehood there were five Baptist churches in the Cumberland basin area, a number deemed sufficient to constitute the Mero Association.

All of the congregations in this association were north of the Cumberland River. But before the end of 1797 three congregations had been organized south of the river — Richland Creek, Mill Creek, and Harpeth. James Whitsett, organizing pastor at Richland Creek, aided in establishing several other churches; and Garner McConnico, who had a reputa-

---

Above: Restored building of Sinking Creek Baptist Church, located between Johnson City and Elizabethton, the oldest surviving Baptist congregation. *Below:* Replica of Strother's Meeting House on the campus on Scarritt College. Originally located in Sumner County, it was the scene of the first Methodist Conference.

tion for "casting out devils," was soon preaching for several congregations along the banks of the Harpeth River after "settling in" as pastor of the Harpeth church.

The types of ministers who served the churches also proved advantageous in fostering the Baptists. They were colorful and interesting individuals, usually licensed or ordained, scattered among the settlers. Licensing, a first step in making a Baptist preacher, was awarded by vote of a local congregation. The licensed preacher usually traveled about preaching to various congregations rather than settling in with a single church. Sometimes a congregation encouraged a good prospect for the ministry to apply for a license to preach. Ordination, a degree higher than licensing, usually took place after a church had "called" a man to be a full-time, settled minister. These men were largely of the "farmer-preacher" variety, individuals who labored during the week and on Sunday preached to attentive congregations. Farmers, blacksmiths, traders —vocations came first; preaching was additional. Energetic, self-supporting, frontier Baptists disapproved of paying a minister; consequently, pastors expected no income from ministerial activities. Any pastor bold enough to mention the matter of compensation had an "outcry against him as a hireling." It was said that the people "loved the gospel, and they loved its ministers, but the sound of money drove all the good feeling from their hearts."

The Baptist pastor had the advantage of coming from the ranks of the people among whom he lived, worked, and preached. He wore the common garb of his fellow citizens. He not only understood the habits, manners, and language of the listeners, but he lived very much in the manner of the people to whom he preached. He knew the lives and problems of his neighbors and was therefore effective.

The lack of education, a matter of little concern either to preacher or congregation, produced an extemporaneous style of preaching. Personal experiences and common sense, not book learning, were the important sermon ingredients. Preaching on the frontier was often noisy, sometimes even wild and incoherent. The emotional discourses were intended to reach the heart of the rugged settlers. The scared, the dissolute, the immoral were reminded that there was a moral principle which challenged and placed a demand upon them. The pastors did not intend to allow any to forget that there was a spiritual presence, even on the frontier, which required of all people their loyalty and their love.

The first resident Baptist pastor in the state, Tidence Lane, was typical of the "farmer-preacher" type. Coming to Tennessee from North

Carolina, Lane led in the establishment of the church at Buffalo Ridge and became the resident pastor. He speculated extensively in purchasing and selling land; at various times he had an income from work as a tax assessor, surveyor, supervisor of road construction, farmer, and custodian of orphans. But he also had time to be a good pastor and probably left a deeper impression upon early Tennessee Baptist life than any other pioneer Baptist minister.

Pastors like Lane placed Baptist activities on a firm footing and were instrumental in bringing into existence a sufficient number of churches to constitute two associations, the Holston and Mero, by the time Tennessee became the sixteenth state to join the nation.

The only other sizeable religious group in the area during this period was the Methodist. By comparison, it arrived late in Tennessee. During the early years of Presbyterian and Baptist activity, the Methodists were still within the Church of England. Methodist societies, made up of those who desired a more personal religious experience than that provided by the ritual of the Anglican church, had existed in the colonies since 1766. It was not until the historic Christmas Conference, meeting in Baltimore in the last week of 1784, severing the societies from the Church of England, that the Methodist Episcopal Church in the United States of America started on its independent way.

Established mainly on the Atlantic Coast, Methodism crept over the Allegheny barrier into Tennessee near the end of the Revolution. Early in 1783 the Holston Conference of Methodist societies was formed, including congregations on the Watauga, Holston, and Nolichucky rivers. Jeremiah Lambert, a traveling preacher from Delaware, arrived to serve this far-flung area. Because of the relation of the societies to the Church of England, prejudice and suspicion hovered over Methodism. Suspected by many Tennesseans of having been too friendly to the British position, the movement experienced no rush of new members. Lambert worked against great odds. Approximately sixty Methodists were on the circuit when he arrived; he was able to add only sixteen new communicants during an entire year of activity. In 1784 Henry Wills succeeded Lambert, but he apparently was unable to increase the membership.

Once Methodism became independent and Americanized, after the 1784 Baltimore conference, success became more evident. The system of classes — embryonic congregations — local leaders, and circuits of classes proved particularly suited to a widely scattered population. The circuit rider, equipped with Bible, hymn book, and John Wesley's sermons, rode the wilderness traces to established settlements and farmsteads pro-

claiming a religious doctrine congenial to the democratic philosophy of the frontier. In 1786, with three circuit riders adding 250 new members, a milestone was attained when Acuff's Chapel, the first Methodist building, was erected near present-day Blountville.

Methodism reached the Cumberland region in 1787, when Benjamin Ogden, a veteran of the Revolutionary War, came down from Kentucky to preach in the settlements. The circuit, which he attempted to cover at least once a month, embraced Nashville and all the forts and communities on the north side of the Cumberland River, as far as Clarksville on the west and Gallatin on the east. Preaching at every opportunity, he slowly gathered converts into classes. These at first, like those in the east, were not churches but simply religious societies, eventually evolving, in most instances, into churches. A grove of trees in the warm months and a convenient home in the winter provided a gathering place. Gradually log chapels were built, followed in time by frame and brick buildings. In 1790, the Methodists erected a stone meeting house in Nashville, between the public square and the river, the "first in the west," and James Robertson, a founder and leading citizen of the town, and his wife joined the movement. In 1795, Absalom Hooper, who lived on White's Creek, a few miles north of Nashville, deeded to Methodist Bishop Francis Asbury "a lot of land on which a church was erected."

When Tennessee attained statehood, Methodism had become established, but with only about 550 members, who were shepherded by four circuit riders in the west and five in the east. These circuit riders, in competition with the Presbyterians and Baptists, labored diligently to increase the numbers.

Considering the physical surroundings, it was remarkable that any of the denominations met with success. It was against almost insurmountable odds that even the smallest gathering of people was possible. That they were able to be maintained, once the decision was reached to organize, is amazing.

There was no means of travel except by walking or riding horseback over hilly, rough, and, in inclement weather, muddy roads. Facilities for communication were meager and crude, as were living accommodations.

Houses, in most instances, were built of round logs. The cracks were chinked and filled with mortar; nevertheless, some large cracks were

Methodist circuit rider, a familiar figure in early Tennessee. Drawing by A.V. Waud, *Harper's Weekly,* Oct. 12, 1867.

usually left that were impossible to fill. Some of the more pretentious houses were built of logs hewn on both sides and carefully notched at the corners. Even a few frame and stone houses began to appear. The roof, generally of "rived" boards, was weighted down with poles. A shingle roof was rare. Chimneys were of wood, lined with stone and mortar, with a deep fireplace at the bottom. Glass windows were almost unknown. Most windows were openings with broad shutters, and when light was desired, the windows, along with the doors, were opened. Only a few of the better houses had plank floors. The dwellings were very small, and many had but one all-purpose room. The furniture was plain but sturdy and usually made by unskilled hands. Structures built for housing the new congregations employed this same type of building construction and furnishings.

The people who occupied these houses and made up the first congregations were the ones who cut down trees, cleared the land, trimmed the logs, made the rails and fences, burned the brush, grubbed the ground, ploughed the fields, planted the crops, reaped the harvest, tended the stores, and taught the children. They wore homespun, home-dyed, home-made clothes, and their shoes, very likely, were of coarse, undressed, unstained red leather. As a rule they ate dark, tough biscuits made from cornmeal and drank coffee, usually sweetened with honey. Of course, some, both male and female, consumed stronger drink on occasion. They ate meats—squirrel, turkey, rabbit, deer, bear, fox, coon, opossum, and bird—which were plentiful, and vegetables, which were difficult to grow. They attended and participated in house raisings, log rollings, corn shuckings, and quiltings. And they made possible the establishment of congregations.

But only barely established! As aggressive as the Methodists, Presbyterians, and Baptists were, they were not overly successful in denting the irreligion of frontier Tennessee. Most of the settlers may have had a nodding acquaintance with religion, but only a few had formal affiliation. As late as 1796, no more than one in twenty identified with any of the three denominations. Out of a population approaching 100,000, fewer than 5,000 held church membership. The Baptists had attracted the largest following with approximately 2,500 members; the Presbyterians had 1,500; and the Methodists fewer than 600.

Uprooted from more normal conditions of life, the new residents, of necessity, had given primary attention merely to surviving. Indifference had emerged as the major attitude toward religion. It characterized the masses. The lack of interest in religion prompted Bishop Francis Asbury, who had visited among Tennessee Methodists as early as 1788, to declare that the settlers had come to the area not to get religion but to get plenty of good land. He predicted that unless the sentiment changed most residents would "eventually lose their souls."

But there was a positive note! The Presbyterians and Baptists, after nearly two decades, and the Methodists after more than a dozen years had established their respective denominations. The seed for the development of Protestantism had been sown!

2. Revivalism

The religious picture was not altogether bright as Tennessee approached the final years of the eighteenth century. Although the denominations that were destined to have the dominant role in the religious life of the state were established, the members they could claim were few and widely scattered. In entire areas there were no churches to attend and Sunday was spent pursuing other interests. The number of clergy was far too meager to add significantly to the membership and give organized religion a vigor and vitality. Church growth lagged far behind growth in population. In 1787 there was a decline in church affiliation in the state from the previous year. The downward trend continued through 1798.

With organized religion stalemated, if not moribund, the baser elements of frontier life appeared to be in unconquerable ascendancy. The scattered villages increasingly became the gathering places of unsavory individuals fleeing the long arm of eastern justice. They had little regard for religion, education, or any cultural enrichment. It was very difficult for even the most dedicated citizens to maintain a proper sense of values over against the large, rowdy element who drank hard liquor as routinely as they ate food and regularly engaged in profane, immoral, and drunken behavior. Lorenzo Dow, an eccentric Methodist Savonarola, probably summarized the opinions of the majority when he declared that Tennessee "was a sink of iniquity, a Black Pit of irreligion."

To add to the bleakness, Deism—a rationalistic faith that revered God for the marvels of His universe rather than for His powers over mankind —had come across the mountains to attack the orthodox Christian concept of God, scoff at the Bible and sacraments, belittle the clergy, and deny the necessity of the church. Considering the literacy rate and the difficulties in communication, it is unlikely that Deism had any significant impact, but it was a lingering threat.

Exasperated, under a cloud of despondency, many ministers, especially the Presbyterians, began to call upon their small congregations to undertake days of fasting and sessions of prayer. They hoped that the fast — a time-honored symbol of forsaking worldliness — and prayer — a call upon God for spiritual aid — would combine to lead to a single-minded devotion to religion. Isolated congregations slowly began to conduct services emphasizing fasting, and hospitable cabins became the scene of prayer meetings in the effort to find meaning and hope in a predicament that offered mainly despair and bewilderment.

Whether in answer to fasting and prayer, or a response to deplorable conditions, or a combination, a period of unusual religious activity began, almost as if by spontaneous combustion. Subsequently labeled the Great Revival in the West, it was actually a massive wave of evangelistic enthusiasm that was to alter the religious configuration in Tennessee.

The revival broke out in neighboring Logan County, Kentucky. The spark that ignited the evangelistic fervor was supplied by the experienced and dramatic Presbyterian evangelist James McGready. A native of Pennsylvania, McGready was described as "exceedingly uncouth in his personal appearance, with small piercing eyes, coarse tremendous voice, and so unusual was his general ugliness as to attract attention." His evangelistic endeavors had brought him notoriety in Pennsylvania and in North Carolina. In South Carolina he had been accused of "running people distracted"; and there developed fierce opposition to him and his preaching. The opposition became so intense — to the extent that a threatening letter was sent to him, written in blood — that he decided to move west. In 1797 he became pastor of three small Presbyterian churches in Logan County: Gasper River, Muddy River, and Red River. For two years, he preached with his usual zeal, but the preaching was not accompanied with the spectacular results his previous efforts had evoked.

But in the summer of 1799 religious interest increased. A service on the last Sunday of July at the Red River church resulted in more than a normal emotional response. And during a meeting in August at Gasper River a small revival developed so suddenly that even McGready was taken by surprise. Conspicuous conversions and uninhibited physical responses attracted attention; religious enthusiasm gained momentum. In late September at the Muddy River church a revival was again experienced and in late October there was a final revival meeting for the year. This time it was in Tennessee at the Presbyterian church in present-day Sumner County where the unusually fervent Presbyterian, William McGee, served as minister. The Sumner County meeting continued the upswing in religious enthusiasm.

PREACHING.

BOARDING TENT.

PRAYER MEETING.

The several small revivals of 1799 had served to increase an interest in religion, but the first extraordinary demonstration of religious fervor came in 1800. In June of that year many members of the three congregations served by McGready gathered at the Red River church for a four-day sacramental meeting. Visiting the service were two Tennessee ministers, William McGee, the Presbyterian, and his brother, John, a Methodist, from Dixon Springs in present-day Smith County. Both were invited to participate in the services. Friday, Saturday, and Sunday services were marked by staid reverence. But Monday, according to McGready, "was indeed the great day of the feast." During a long service, a woman began to shout and sing. She stopped as abruptly as she had begun; the ministers concluded the service and prepared to leave the building. The McGee brothers, however, along with most of the congregation, not yet satisfied with the results of the service, did not move. William, filled with religious excitement, rose to speak but, overcome with emotion, sat on the floor weeping. Immediately, many in the congregation began to sob. Trembling, John McGee stood, and with uncontrolled fervor began to exhort the crowd, telling them the Holy Spirit was present. Cries and shouts broke out among the congregation. John McGee moved through the building shouting and exhorting with tremendous ecstasy and energy. The floor was soon covered with those who had been singed by his religious fire and who had fallen in a state of semi-consciousness.

News spread rapidly of the occurrences at Red River. Capitalizing on the publicity, McGready immediately made plans for another sacramental meeting, this one to be held at the Gasper River church the last weekend in July.

By early Friday of the announced weekend, unprecedented crowds began congregating at Gasper River. "The high number in attendance, their interdenominational nature, and the general air of anticipation infused the scene with a kind of intuitive awareness that this was to be a special occasion." Abruptly on Saturday night, after two days of preaching, "the divine flame spread through the whole multitude" and people were "lying powerless in every part of the house, praying and crying for mercy." The Presbyterian and Methodist ministers worked through the night and into Sunday morning as pinched spirits and starved souls

Above: A typical scene during the Great Revival. *Below*: A prayer meeting.

found relief. Both young and old were caught up by the enthusiasm and converted in great numbers. Occurring in a time and place of religious bareness, the events at Gasper River began to be interpreted as heralding the religious awakening for which much praying and fasting had been undertaken.

As accounts grew of the soul-stirring moans of convictions and the joyous shouts of comforting conversions, the Gasper River meeting became the catalytic agent that set off other similar revivals.

After witnessing the success of McGrady's meeting at Gasper River, William McGee returned home to Sumner County determined to try a similar method. There had been scattered outcroppings of localized revival fervor in Tennessee before McGee made plans for his meeting. Gideon Blackburn had carefully promoted a reawakening of religious commitment among Presbyterians in Blount County in the spring of 1800. A fiery Methodist, John Page, had successfully stoked the smoldering religious zeal of several Cumberland settlements. And in Sumner County the coals burst into flame. In mid-summer 1800, a group from the Shiloh Presbyterian Church made the short trip to Gasper River. Upon returning home to Sumner County, they described what they interpreted to be the work of God at Gasper River. The reports generated tremendous religious enthusiasm. At a September sacramental service at Desha's Creek, near Shiloh, a crowd of unprecedented size appeared and many "fell like corn before a storm of wind." Both William and John McGee, James McGready, and other Presbyterian and Methodist ministers took part. The peculiar emotional responses that had taken place at Gasper River reoccurred at the Desha's Creek services. To the participants, the emotional exercises seemed to authenticate the work.

A month later, William McGee began a planned five-day meeting at Drake's Creek, also in Sumner County. He was assisted by four other Presbyterian ministers; over a thousand people were in attendance. The meeting had the same emotional responses at Gasper River and Desha's Creek. On the last day there was added excitement when Methodist Bishops Francis Asbury and Richard Whatcoat, along with William McKendree, a Methodist presiding elder, visited the site. They were asked to participate; all three preached to the assembly. In his journal, Bishop Asbury described the concluding service: "The ministers of God, Methodists and Presbyterians, united their labours, and mingled with the childlike simplicity of primitive times. Fires blazing here and there dispelled the darkness, and the shouts of the redeemed captives, and the cries of precious souls struggling into life, broke the silence of midnight."

The bishop was moved to add that at Drake's Creek "heaven

Winter postponed additional meetings, but spring brough
sphere of expectancy. Soon settlements throughout the Cumberland re
gion began reporting awakenings. The religious news emanating from
the revival centers generated additional awakenings. By late summer,
the Baptists had joined with the Presbyterians and Methodists to hold
one successive emotional revival after another; crowds approaching
5,000 were frequent. The revival spread like an epidemic; from one rural
community to another, religious excitement increased until the entire
state seemed at fever pitch. No sooner did enthusiasm wane in one settlement than it erupted in one or more other locations. Meetings that
customarily had lasted for days began to go on for weeks. Worshipers
exceeded the capacity of any building, and services were moved outdoors. Excitement and tension mounted. Day and night, ministers and
converts rushed about praying and exhorting. When one preacher became exhausted, another took his place; in the larger assemblies as many
as six or seven would be speaking at the same time, keeping alive the momentum. Even when the preachers concluded, the services frequently
were carried on by the laity — men, women, and children — who exhorted,
prayed, and wept. There was scarcely a moment devoid of activity. Unlike the still small voice, or gently flowing water, the revival resembled a
whirlwind, an earthquake, a tempestuous torrent.

The tremendous excitement that characterized the revival in Tennessee was accompanied by strange manifestations never before witnessed
in the area. Reasonable decorum marked the revival in the beginning,
but as it gained momentum, some fantastic and fanatical demonstrations
emerged. This "acrobatic Christianity" — a raw, emotional response that
resembled some kind of convulsive seizure, sometimes resulting from
deliberate manipulations by the evangelists — was always encouraged by
the highly charged atmosphere.

The "falling exercise" was the most common of all forms of bodily excitement. Amid sobs, moans, cries, some worshipers would be struck
down with violent motions of the body. Those who fell would sometimes
lie for hours helpless and apparently unconscious of what was going on
around them; when they recovered from their trance-like state it was
with exclamations of joy and praise. Most were struck down at the meetings, but some fell on their way home, or while working in the fields.
One unbeliever, who had boasted he would not fall and attempted to
prove that the fallen were shamming, was struck down and when able to
speak "acknowledged himself a great sinner."

The "jerking exercise" was also quite common and was the one that spread most rapidly through a congregation. Even preachers were not immune. The jerking exercise affected different persons in different ways. Frequently only one of the limbs would be involved, sometimes the whole body, and often only the head alone. Occasionally those who were seized would be thrown violently to the ground, yet they reported the experience to be one of the happiest of their lives. Peter Cartwright, noted frontier Methodist preacher, recollected that he had seen more than 500 persons jerking at one time; among them were ornately dressed young men and women whose fine bonnets, caps, and combs "were hurled through the air by the jerking of the head."

Related to falling and jerking were rolling, running, dancing, and barking exercises. The barking exercise, where persons went down on all fours and barked until they grew hoarse, made a lasting impression. It was not uncommon to see people gathered around a tree, barking, yelping, "treeing the devil." The name of this exercise originated when a Presbyterian minister in East Tennessee got the jerks and grasped a tree for support. A punster who saw him in that position reported he had found the clergyman "barking up a tree."

The bizarre physical phenomena and the excessive emotionalism were produced in part by the emotional oratory of the evangelists, reinforced by hymns of challenge and warning. But the discourses that aided in creating the highly charged atmosphere were not all heat and no light. William McGee and other Presbyterians attempted to create a revivalism with a theology based on their Calvinistic training. This stance, however, was badly compromised; modified Calvinism made fairly peaceful accommodation with the ascendancy of Methodist Arminianism. The doctrine consisted of the preaching of potential universal redemption, free and full salvation, justification by faith, regeneration by the Holy Spirit, and the joy of a living religion. Theological differences were reduced to a minimum to encourage cooperation. Often it was more the method used to convey the message, rather than the message itself that created the effect.

In Tennessee, the revival developed a new and unique institution—the camp meeting. Probably the most striking manifestation of the Great Revival, it was born of the necessities of frontier conditions. Because people had to travel great distances to reach the place where religious services

---

Above: The camp meeting, a new and unique institution that developed in Tennessee during the Great Revival. *Below*: A prayer meeting.

were held, they could not leave early enough to return home the same night. So they adopted the practice of bringing provisions and equipment for camping on the spot, with plans to stay for several days. There had been large overnight religious gatherings before, but the people had been lodged in inadequate neighborhood facilities rather than involved in an activity that combined the pleasure of camping with a religious service.

The first camp meeting in Tennessee, at Desha's Creek in Sumner County, in August 1800, was under the sponsorship of John McGee, the Smith County Methodist generally acclaimed "the father of camp meetings in America." The planned practice of camping out for the continuous outdoor services became popular and powerful. The new religious device, with its sociability, its simplicity, its emotional magnetism, transmitted through days of fervent exhorting, group singing, shouting, and praying, found ready acceptance. Encampment after encampment, well-publicized, drew huge crowds as Methodists, Presbyterians, and, somewhat reluctantly, Baptists united to hold one highly charged revival after another through the remainder of the summer and fall of 1800 and, after a winter pause, throughout the warm weather of 1801.

At camp meeting time, homes were temporarily deserted, stores were closed, business was suspended, and crops were left untended in the fields. "Bold hunters and sober matrons, young men, maidens, and little children flocked to the common center of attraction; every difficulty was surmounted; every risk ventured, to be present at the holy fair."

At first sight, the camp meeting presented a scene of confusion. Free of the restraints of a formal meeting house, the religious activity was largely unplanned and service routines were often quite spontaneous. Since this was a social as well as a religious occasion, competing with the religious activities of singing, preaching, and praying and with the responsive sobs, shrieks, shouts, sudden spasms, and seizures was the sight of spectators casually walking about, talking, and laughing freely.

With such large crowds assembled in the open air under circumstances of unusually peculiar excitement, there was bound to be some disorder, some mingling of "human passions not sanctified by grace." A critic of the revivals stated that acts of immorality took place on the camp grounds under the cover of darkness, or in the neighboring forest. He observed that while the religious services were going on within the camp, "all manner of wickedness was going on without." To prevent irregularities, misconduct, and moral laxity, the use of vigilance committees and a set of regulations became necessary.

The camp meetings in Tennessee made marked impressions upon numerous participants. Thousands were deeply moved; a large number professed conversion and many, whose religious beliefs had been only nominal, found their faith invigorated. While the camp meetings continued to be a part of the scene for many years, the revival movement they nurtured peaked about 1805 and steadily declined after that.

But before the movement was spent, the Great Revival established religious concepts that undergirded and characterized religion in Tennessee for decades to come. It also provided an impetus that set the three major denominations on a path of unprecedented growth.

The evangelical religion that had captured the popular mind was to be an individual matter, a thing of the heart. Sermons were aimed at individual sinners. While there were social reforms, ministers called persons, not society, to account for their transgressions. Emphasis was on individual Christian living after conversion. This concept shaped most religious activity.

Of the three denominations, the Methodist benefited most from the revival. Although revivalism had been mainly sponsored by the Presbyterians in its initial stages, Methodists had been the most enthusiastic participants, reaping the largest number of church members. A converted person did not automatically become a church member; he was won by persuasion to a specific denomination, and no one was more persuasive than a Methodist.

Building on the foundation provided by revivalism, the Methodist church shrewdly and readily adapted its program to the frontier. After the Presbyterians and Baptists withdrew their cooperation, the Methodists continued to make use of camp meetings to preach the "doctrine of the Bible in the Arminian view of those doctrines." This "view" placed emphasis on free will — self-determination — and minimized theological expectations. An effective organization, including the circuit system and clergymen who gave themselves to full-time religious activity, was an additional advantage.

The system of circuits, devised by John Wesley and brought to America by Francis Asbury, was ideally suited for Tennessee's scattered population. A circuit involved as much as 500 miles and took five to six weeks for a minister to cover. Held in cabins, sheds, taverns, under trees, in the open, there was usually a service somewhere on the circuit every day. Between visits by the circuit rider, a layman, designed to be the class leader, gave spiritual direction to the class, which seldom numbered more than twenty persons.

The generally young, unmarried, uneducated, zealous circuit riders, later frequently referred to as "God's shock troops," had a major role in the success of Methodism. Out in all kinds of weather, seldom assured of a place to spend the night, they were often sickly, and many died. "There is nothing out today but crows and Methodist preachers" grew into a proverbial saying. To be a circuit rider was to take a vow of poverty, but, as Bishop Asbury declared, they "were rich in the faith." Wearing a double-breasted black coat, short black breeches, long stockings, with hair parted in the middle and hanging long to the shoulders, to "accentuate the sanctified look," a circuit rider was easy to spot. The pressures of time and lack of education produced a clergy that gave simple, direct sermons. Many Tennesseans responded to them by joining the Methodist church.

Supervisory clergymen, then called "presiding elders," also had a significant role in Methodism's success. The superintendent who most significantly influenced the development of Methodism in Tennessee, as he led the circuit riders in carrying the gospel to homes and churches, was William McKendree. A native of Virginia, of limited education, an early convert to Methodism, McKendree came to the West in 1800, at age fifty-three, to supervise the Methodist work in the Western District, which included Tennessee. For eight years he was the field marshal, organizing new circuits and either finding or developing preachers to man them. Following his election as bishop in 1808, he established his base in Nashville and was a familiar figure among Tennessee Methodists until his death in 1835.

On the eve of the Great Revival, shortly before McKendree became associated with Methodism in Tennessee, there were approximately 600 members in the state; in 1800 the denomination counted over 10,000 members and 25 clergymen, constituting the largest religious body in the state.

In 1812, the Methodist church, along with other denominations, experienced an astonishing increase in membership, and for an unusual reason. Natural phenomena in the form of a comet and a series of earthquakes increased religious enthusiasm. The earthquakes, causing vibrations that continued for weeks and creating Reelfoot Lake in northwest Tennessee, were interpreted by many persons to be a "direct agency of Jehovah." Three times, between December 1811 and February 1812, major quakes jolted the region; credulous people read the wrath of God into every quake. Peter Cartwright was in Nashville when the first severe

---

Peter Cartwright, popular frontier Methodist preacher.

shock from the earthquakes was felt. He saw a woman start to the spring for water. When the earth began to tremble and the chimneys and scaffolding around buildings being erected began to fall, she shouted: "The Lord is coming in the clouds of Heaven! The day of judgment is here." It was a time of widespread terror, and in deep fear many sought to right their sinful ways. Settlers, hastening to atone for their past, sought grace with religious fervor and devotion. While many hearts were faint and fear was rampant, preachers made use of the catastrophes of nature. Like the Nashville woman, they declared the end of the world was at hand, and a person's only hope lay in baptism and church membership. Many preachers were besieged by a "terror stricken crowd" to preach. Preach they did, reaping a bountiful harvest for their churches. In the one year, Methodist membership increased by 50 percent. Because so many joined from fright and terror, a number of ministers rightly had misgivings concerning the permanency of some of the conversions.

The beginning of the war with England in the summer of 1812 suddenly checked membership growth. Methodism, along with other denominations, lost much of what it gained through the earthquakes and general religious zeal. As the martial spirit flamed, people seemed to lose their "zeal for the cause of God." Membership declined through 1815.

Methodism was able to grow again when West Tennessee, formerly called "Indian Country," was opened up for settlement in 1819. The region, with no roads and not a single community, had been a vast hunting ground. Differing from East and Middle Tennessee, the settlement of West Tennessee was rapid. The total strength of the Tennessee Conference, formed in 1816 and including all of Tennessee and about half of Kentucky, was thrown into evangelizing the area. The going was rough during the formative years, but the circuit riders were equal to the opportunity. Arthur Davis, one of the first on the scene, is an example. On his initial trip to the preaching point, Davis was met by a band of raiders, one of whom announced that "no damned Methodist preacher should preach." Davis completely disregarded the threat and preached. At the close of the service he turned to his adversaries and said, "I am now ready to meet you." So unexpected was this boldness and courage that the spokesman for the group threw down his club and said, "You're my sort of man . . . you shall preach here whenever it may please you to do so, and I will see you do it in peace." With such support and protection it is not surprising that the growth of Methodism in West Tennessee was rapid. After two years there were almost 10,000 members. With West Tennessee's population increasing in the ten years after 1820 by ap-

proximately 140,000, there were more prospects for membership than
ever before. The Methodists became too numerous to be cared for adequately by one conference; in 1824 the state was divided into the Holston and Tennessee conferences, and although other states were partially
included, the vast portion of the strength was in Tennessee. By 1830
there were approximately 35,000 Methodists in Tennessee, making it by
far the state's largest denomination.

Success in acquiring numbers seemed to make the Methodists more
sectarian. Although they had cooperated during the revival, the Methodists now vied with the Presbyterians and Baptists. In an aggressive
search for additions, the Methodists turned attention to converting the
same people in whom the Baptists were interested. As they lined up as
the chief contenders for converts, the two denominations, eying each
other suspiciously, developed attitudes of extreme antagonism and tore
into each other's ranks with abandon, casting aside all courtesy and
ethics. The Methodists sang:

> I'll tell you who the Lord loves best —
> It is the shouting Methodist!

The Baptists replied:

> Baptist, Baptist, Baptist —
> Baptist till I die.
> I'll go along with the Baptists
> And find myself on High.

The sacrament of Baptism was one area of conflict; the Methodists,
who baptized by sprinkling, heaped ridicule on the Baptists — who prac-
ticed immersion — for their doctrine of the regenerative power of water.
The communion service was also the object of disagreement. The Baptists, "who broke bread and sipped the wine with none but the Baptists,
and not all of them," were blasted by the Methodists when the Baptists
prohibited their members from attending the popular love feasts of the
Methodists, which generally involved an open communion service. But
the Methodists did not expend all of their ammunition on the Baptists;
they constantly put the Presbyterians on the defensive. On one occasion
Peter Cartwright, in an effort to establish a Methodist church near
present-day Hendersonville, assaulted the beliefs of the Presbyterians —
who worshiped in a small building across from where he preached — with
such force that, of the the twenty-seven persons who formed the new
Methodist congregation, thirteen had come from the Presbyterian church.

As a result, the Presbyterian minister was forced to move to Missouri.

No voice of prejudice was louder than that of "Parson" William G. Brownlow, a controversial East Tennessee Methodist. When several nondenominational agencies, such as the American Bible Society and the American Tract Society, attempted to work in Tennessee, Brownlow violently opposed them, alleging that they were under the control of the Presbyterians. Other Methodists joined Brownlow's attacks and the agencies were not able to gain immediate entry into the state. As late as 1845, the Presbyterian Synod of Tennessee had to deal with the attack and the "too successful misrepresentation of the doctrines and polity of Presbyterianism made by the Methodists."

The Baptists, in strong competition with the Methodists, became reluctant participants in the Great Revival. The early camp meetings sponsored by the Presbyterians and Methodists had some Baptists taking part. The extravagances of the revival created a decided distaste among the Baptists, but no group could stand aloof and retain its membership against the headlong sweep of the movement. The Baptists simply became less and less involved in the cooperative ventures and changed the channel of revivalism from a camp meeting to a Baptist "protracted meeting." As a rule, at the protracted meetings there was no overnight camping, but the tactics varied little from those of the camp meeting.

In 1801 and 1802, Baptist churches in the state that had not received anyone by baptism for a year or more began to baptize as many as twenty converts during the course of a protracted meeting. In the Holston Association, for example, 27 churches reported 59 additions in 1800; in 1802, 36 churches reported 793 baptisms. Not only were there new members, but there were also new churches. Even more impressive results were reported in the Cumberland area, the scene of the most intense revivalism. But while the Baptist "farmer-preachers" labored diligently, they did not have the success of the Methodist circuit riders in gaining members. The increase in Baptist membership was only about half that of the Methodists during the early years of the nineteenth century. The opportunities for the Baptists to overtake the Methodists, especially when West Tennessee was opened up for evangelistic enterprise in 1819, were constantly retarded by internal controversies that dissipated energies in unproductive strife.

One of the earliest Baptist controversies arose in 1814 over the efforts to bring about a statewide organization. This did not sit well with congregations that thought of each individual church as a separate, distinct, autonomous unit. They saw in the Tennessee Baptist Meeting of Correspondents the beginning of "papacy" and the decline of local autonomy. Baptists enjoyed their freedom too much and feared any attempt at organization which might in any way transgress that freedom. At any proposal suggesting organization, they came out fighting.

In 1816, Tennessee Baptists were at odds among themselves over the issue of missions. Some members in the Concord Association, in the Cumberland region, made known plans to form a missionary society. Daniel Parker, a native of Virginia who arrived in the state in 1803 and soon became an implacable foe of missions in any form, made a slashing attack on missionary societies as money-grabbing devices wholly contrary to the Baptist system. He threatened to "burst the Association" if it continued any semblance of missionary activity.

The same year the Tennessee Association, in East Tennessee, after a visit by Luther Rice, a noted Baptist missionary, took steps to organize a missionary society. But Parker attacked the proposal and again charged that missions constituted nothing more than a scheme for collecting money for an unworthy group of men. He coupled his opposition to societies with opposition to ministerial education; and traveling widely, preaching incessantly, and writing a stream of pamphlets and books, he was effective in bringing many missionary societies to dissolution and many programs to an end. John Taylor, a Kentucky Baptist minister, and Alexander Campbell, during this period a Baptist minister residing in present-day West Virginia, aided Parker in sowing anti-missionary sentiment.

Hardly a Baptist church or an association escaped internal troubles over missions. The anti-mission triumph in Tennessee was striking. A contemporary wrote that the negative sentiment had swollen until no one dared resist it. He declared: "Not a man ventured to open his mouth in favor of any benevolent enterprise. The missionary societies were dissolved, and the associations rescinded all their resolutions by which they were in any way connected with the measures." The anti-missions movement adversely affected the growth and progress of Baptist work in the state for many years.

In addition to controversies over organizations and missionary societies, there were internal doctrinal disturbances which plagued the Baptists and limited their efforts to secure new members. Probably the most interesting one involved Reuben Ross, a popular Montgomery County preacher. Ross, a native of North Carolina, moved to that county in 1808 and helped organize the Spring Creek Baptist Church, serving as its pastor for almost thirty years. He had been reared to believe in "limited atonement" and had been held to the concept that since Christ died for the "elect" only, the gospel was not to be preached to convert sinners but to comfort and encourage the "saved." Ross became the most popular and influential preacher of this doctrine, held by most of the Baptists in Montgomery County. Exposed to revival influences, he gradually changed his theological position and in 1817 began preaching "unlimited atonement" and declared that salvation was for all who repented and became followers of Christ. Charges were brought against Ross and a heated controversy developed. It climaxed in 1827, when churches supporting the new doctrinal position of Ross withdrew from the Red River Association and formed the Bethel Association.

More detrimental to the Baptists than the controversy centering around Reuben Ross was the one that focused on the teaching and activity of Alexander Campbell. Campbell, a former Presbyterian who began an uneasy affiliation with the Baptists in 1813, became the leader of a new religious movement when the Mahoning Baptist Association, located mainly in Ohio, voted in 1830 to dissolve as a Baptist body and took on the name "Reformers." The Reformers, who had been advocating Christian unity through the restoration of New Testament Christianity for several years before the action of the Mahoning Association, inspired a number of other Baptist associations, especially in Kentucky, to vote themselves out of existence and become affiliated with the new movement.

Tennessee was exposed to the Reformers when Philip Fall moved to Nashville from Louisville to teach at the Nashville Female Academy. When Fall arrived, the First Baptist Church was without a pastor, and Fall, who had led the first Baptist Church at Louisville into the Reformers camp before coming to Nashville, was called as temporary pastor. He lost no time in taking the Nashville church into the Campbell fold.

In Middle Tennessee, the Baptists lost heavily to the Reformers. The Concord Association, for example, was reduced from 49 churches with 3,399 members to 11 churches with 805 members. The drain from Baptist membership became more pronounced when the Reform movement merged with the Christian Church in 1832, to be known variously as the Christian Church, the Disciples of Christ, and the Churches of Christ. The new sect proselytized members also from the Methodist and Presbyterian churches, but the gains were never as significant as those from the Baptists. The practice of immersion, the emphasis on local autonomy, and Campbell's personal magnetism, along with his dedication to restoring New Testament Christianity, were features that had a special appeal to Baptists.

Controversy distracted the Baptists in efforts to steadily increase membership rolls, but it did not deter them from "turning out" wayward members who were already in the fold. To maintain a committed membership was more important than having a large membership. The Baptists became the most vigilant of the denominations in supervising the moral and general conduct of members. A Baptist congregation in assembly frequently took the place of a grand jury and dealt with both sacred and secular items. Failure to attend church services regularly, "communing with other denominations," "holding erroneous doctrines," and fornication nearly always led to removal. Various cases of lying, stealing, fraud, and dishonesty fell under the alert eye of the church. Many churches customarily cleared the rolls of those who gambled, played cards, drank excessively, or fought. The churches had strong confidence in their disciplinary powers and recognized few limitations to their jurisdiction. The Baptist churches sternly prohibited members from having recourse to law under any circumstances. Lawsuits were regarded as strictly contrary to the teachings of the Baptist gospel, and to bring one was itself a cause for dismissal.

Dismissals, distractions, and disturbances did not prevent the Baptists from making significant gains. While the growth lagged behind that of the Methodists, there were 17,500 Baptists in the state in 1830.

The Presbyterian, the largest denomination on the eve of the Great Revival, was the least successful in taking advantage of the religious enthusiasm provided by revivalism. Ironically, the movement that began among the Presbyterians was responsible for eventually tearing the denomination apart, leaving it the weakest and smallest of the three major religious bodies in the state.

Tennessee Presbyterians, spurred by the lethargy of the churches and the great immoralities of the frontier, had been early and eager participants in the Great Revival. As late as 1803, Presbyterians generally felt there was evidence to show the revival was the "work of God." By 1805, however, belief was widespread that the emotional excesses and bodily exercises had tarnished the glory of what, in its first stages, had been so highly promising.

Gradually, Presbyterian ministers who had taken the lead ceased participation as extreme emotional excesses became evident; the theological emphasis turned too drastically in the direction of Arminianism, and cooperation among all of the denominations was deemed absolutely necessary. The distinctiveness of the Presbyterian church was threatened. Some of the older leaders were determined that the denomination would not change its tenets radically or alter its ecclesiastical structure to meet, what they considered, a temporary frontier condition. The Presbyterian structure, as they revered it, could not survive if the forces emanating from the revival were successful in the adoption of a less rigid theology and less stringent rules.

As the older ministers withdrew, younger clerics, more likely to break with their historical theology and dilute Calvinism with doses of free will, moved into leadership roles. This was especially true in the Cumberland region, where the revivals had first appeared and the fervor continued unabated. The multitude of conversions prompted a search for ways to keep the revival fires aglow. To serve the new churches and enlarged congregations, the need for additional ministers became an overriding concern. An expedient remedy was suggested: the local presbytery should lower the educational requirements for the ministery and allow unordained exhorters to perform semiclerical duties. In 1802, the Transylvania Presbytery, which included the Cumberland region, lowered the educational requirements and accepted four men as exhorters. Within a month, a Cumberland presbytery was constituted. Formed from a geographical division of the Transylvania Presbytery and containing all of the Presbyterian churches in present-day Middle Tennessee, the new presbytery immediately began to license and then ordain men who lacked the required educational qualifications for the Presbyterian ministry. The acts of the two presbyteries, for all purposes, divided the Presbyterians into revival and anti-revival factions.

As the newly licensed and ordained ministers, burning with zeal, traveled incessantly, they proclaimed a theology that lodged about midway between the two extremes of Calvinism and Arminianism. Revivalists were called "illiterate exhorters with Arminian sentiments" by the strict Presbyterians, who were determined to make doctrine an issue of intense controversy. It was an issue immediately joined by a related one, the rights and powers of symbols and presbyteries in the theological examination of ministers.

All these issues came to a head when the Kentucky Synod, formed in 1802, after a series of unfortunate blunders, appointed a commission to examine the affairs of the Cumberland Presbytery. Assembling at the Gasper River Meeting House in late December 1805, the synodical commission immediately clashed with the presbytery. Both claimed final jurisdiction in examining candidates for the ministry. The moderator of the commission urged the "suspect ministers" to submit to an examination for synodical approval. They refused. Determined to uphold the supremacy of the synod, the commission suspended these men and several others and prohibited them from performing ministerial functions. The presbytery responded by urging the ministers to continue functioning to keep the churches and revivals alive. Efforts were made at reconciliation, but the synod, in no mood to compromise, declared the Cumberland Presbytery dissolved in 1806, attaching its church members to the Transylvania Presbytery. The Cumberland Presbytery appealed the matter to the General Assembly, which at first attempted to mediate differences but eventually, acting contrary to Presbyterian rules and customs, supported the actions of the synod. In 1809, the revivalists, working to remain within Presbyterianism, made a final effort at reconciliation with the synod. The synod rejected the effort, agreeing only to restore those ministers who would submit to synod requirements. Only three ministers—Finis Ewing, Samuel McAdow, and Samuel King—refused the synod's demands. For all intents and purposes they had renounced the authority of the Presbyterian church. T.C. Anderson, prominent East Tennessee Presbyterian, called Ewing, McAdow, and King "three ignorant boys" who "had put to sea without chart or compass."

Ewing, McAdow, and King—the only ordained ministers who remained faithful to the stand taken by the revivalist element in Presbyterianism—met in the home of McAdow in Dickson County, on February 4, 1810, and constituted the independent Cumberland Presbytery. Not intended as a new church or even a schism, the new presbytery—which stood by the Westminster Confession of the Presbyterians, with some alterations—formed the nucleus for the Cumberland Presbyterian Church, the first denomination to be organized in Tennessee.

The Cumberland region was a fertile field for the growth of the new group. Under the able leadership of Finis Ewing, the "Cumberlands" modified Calvinistic doctrine, adopted a revivalistic program, made use of the camp meeting, and took advantage of the circuit rider system. Growth was phenomenal. Mainline Presbyterianism, which lost heavily to the new church, inadvertently assisted in the growth; a diligent attack by circulars and pamphlets to warn people, instead of hindering, only spurred the rapidly growing Cumberland movement. In three years the Cumberland church had sixty congregations. By 1829 it was large enough to justify a general assembly. Meanwhile, mainline Presbyterianism had fewer than 5,000 adherents in Tennessee.

At about the same time that the Cumberland Presbyterian division was in process and for the same reasons, there was another departure from the Presbyterian fold in the area northeast of Lexington, Kentucky. In 1803, five ministers and several congregations withdrew from

the Synod of Kentucky and constituted themselves as the independent Springfield Presbytery. A year later the presbytery, in a semihumorous document, "The Last Will and Testament of the Springfield Presbytery," voted to dissolve. The several Presbyterian churches in Kentucky and southern Ohio that had made up the presbytery began to use the name Christian Church. When Barton W. Stone, the accepted leader of the new movement, moved to Mansker Creek, not far from present-day Hendersonville, Tennessee, in late 1812, he began to organize Christian Churches in Tennessee. His first efforts were in Sumner and Wilson counties. Stone had visited in the area before, while a Presbyterian minister; and among those who responded to his preaching and organizational endeavors were a number of Presbyterians. Stone remained in Tennessee for two years. Patterning his activities along the line of Methodist circuit riders, some trips took him as far as Rutherford County, and eventually to Maury and Marshall counties, as he personally laid the foundation for the Christian Church in Tennessee.

Of course, the Cumberland Presbyterians and the Christian Church did not monopolize the religious field, but they did play havoc with the Presbyterians. Once the revivalistic element was removed, that denomination had no aggressive programs available to seek and convert the unchurched. The Presbyterian ministers, in their formal way, appeared satisfied to look only for Presbyterians who moved into the communities and who would conform to the doctrine and discipline of the denomination. Most Presbyterians appeared content with the peculiarities of their church. The losses would have been greater had it not been for a few diligent ministers like Gideon Blackburn. Blackburn preached far and wide to prevent defections and worked unceasingly to establish new congregations in strategic places like Franklin, Murfreesboro, and Nashville.

In summary, the activity of the revival and immediate post-revival period literally gave birth to religion in the state. As latent beliefs were awakened and thousands brought into church membership, revivalism placed evangelical religion on such a sound footing that conservative Protestantism, especially that of the Baptists and Methodists, would

---

Above: The home of Samuel McAdow, in Dickson County, where the Cumberland Presbyterian Church was organized. *Below*: Mill Creek Baptist Church, Nashville, where the first Baptist state convention was organized in 1833.

dominate in Tennessee, without serious challenge from any form of liberal or non-Protestant religious groups. The preaching that primarily called persons only, rather than society, to account for their transgressions spawned a practical theology based on individual spiritual experience. Basically Arminian in type, this theology never reached systematic expression, mainly because adherents were too busy practicing it. Unorganized and unexplicated, it found expression in personal pietistic living. Less significant, but important, the measured success of the Great Revival established revivals and protracted meetings as a major force in Tennessee religion, recurring periodically, energizing and enlarging evangelical Protestantism.

3. Maturing Denominations

Most of the early congregations in Tennessee, regardless of denomination, had been established irregularly and spasmodically. Isolated and alone, they had little, if any, relationships across congregational lines, even among the highly structured Presbyterians and Methodists. There were the indefinable ties to certain personalities, but these were confined to specific areas. A minister who served more than one congregation was instrumental in informing one congregation about the other, but this was casual and did not contribute to any real sense of fellowship. Hardly any involvement in common endeavors existed beyond the local organization. There was little sense of unity. Loyalty to a demonination was difficult to ascertain, and defections were commonplace. Except for the Presbyterians, no denomination possessed a unified doctrinal stance.

As the rough edges of frontier life were smoothed and shifting settlers evolved into a stable population, religious leaders, bent on strengthening and giving identity to their particular denominations, turned attention to the difficulties posed by this ambitious goal. The result was an immediate endeavor to tighten denominational lines, primarily through the development of more inclusive organizational structures, the initiation of religious journals to inform the individual members, and the establishment of educational enterprises to train a more enlightened leadership. There was intense activity in these areas throughout the three decades prior to the Civil War.

In efforts to get the congregations inclined toward denominationalism, primary attention focused on organization. Within Methodism the main difficulty was in structuring the denomination rapidly enough to give adequate attention to the increasing number of new members and inculcating in them a denominational loyalty. As quarterly conferences, with jurisdiction over a circuit or station, kept growing in numbers, additional districts were formed, and pressure mounted to increase the number of conferences. Attempts to respond to the religious needs and give adequate supervision to denominational interests were evidenced primarily in the readjustment of conference boundaries.

The Tennessee Conference, including other states besides Tennessee, was organized by Bishop Francis Asbury and Bishop William McKendree, in 1812, at a meeting near present-day Portland, Tennessee. Later the territory was reduced to include only Tennessee and part of Kentucky. In 1820 the territory was again reduced to include only Methodists in Tennessee; these were organized into four districts. The Holston and French Broad districts were removed four years later from the Tennessee Conference, and by expanding and renaming the districts in the area, the Holston Conference in East Tennessee came into being. The rapid growth of Methodism in the western part of the state made an additional conference necessary; so, in 1840 the Memphis Conference was organized. There were no adjustments in these three conferences, embracing all Methodism in the state, until 1844, when the controversy over slavery divided the denomination nationally.

Unlike the Methodists, the Presbyterians, in attempting denominational effectiveness, discovered organization to be a matter of consolidation rather than expansion. The Synod of Tennessee, containing four presbyteries, was formed in 1817 and remained unaltered for about a decade. In 1826 the synod was divided, with the Synod of West Tennessee, containing four presbyteries, formed from it. These new formations, however, did not result from a significant increase in members. Instead they were simply an expedient to reduce the geographical area embraced by a presbytery and bring a greater denominational sensitivity to the member congregations. With but one exception, there were not more than 15 congregations and 10 ministers in any presbytery. New members seldom exceeded 30 annually in any of the presbyteries. For example, in 1834, the Synod of Tennessee, including East Tennessee, where Presbyterianism had been the first denomination on the scene, reported only 64 churches, fewer than 6,000 members, one presbytery having no additions and another having only 8. Both synods remained static for a long period.

Meanwhile, by contrast the Cumberland Presbyterian denomination experienced an impressive growth in numbers and organizations. In 1817 the Cumberland Presbyterians had three presbyteries. Expanding westward, with each congregation almost entirely missionary in purpose and activity, the young denomination reported over 1,100 new members in 1819, over 2,500 in each of the next three years, and by 1825 more than 4,000 annually. At the time of their first General Assembly, in

1829, the Cumberland Presbyterians had the bulk of their organizations and members in Tennessee, which six years later accounted for over 17,000 communicants in 35 presbyteries. Growth continued steadily and rapidly until on the eve of the Civil War an estimated 35,000 Cumberland Presbyterians resided in Tennessee.

The Baptists, with heavy emphasis on local church autonomy, had the greatest difficulty in attaining a denominational posture through organization. Baptist associations, made up of congregations in a geographical area, had existed in Tennessee since 1786. Disavowing any authority over local churches, associations — comprised of representatives from member congregations — usually assumed some responsibility for oversight of struggling churches and rendered services in an advisory capacity, especially when church quarrels developed. Membership growth and the multiplication of Baptist churches, especially during the Great Revival, resulted in a steady organization of new associations. While each functioned independently of the other, a desire arose for a connecting link among them.

The first suggestion to bring the associations together into a statewide organization was made in 1814. Motivated by the formation of the initial national organization of Baptists, the Triennial Convention at Philadelphia, the Concord Association, made up for the most part of Wilson County congregations, advocated the Tennessee Baptist Meeting of Correspondents. But because the agency was to be concerned primarily with missionary programs, the anti-mission forces rallied and were instrumental in having the proposal turned down by the churches.

Once kindled, the flame of anti-missions grew brighter. It absorbed Baptist energies and hardly a congregation or association escaped internal difficulty over the issue. The anti-missions movement, which also denounced Sunday schools and Bible societies, reflected an intense opposition to any ecclesiastical authority and brought bitterness and division. But this disarray, followed by large defections led by Alexander Campbell, prompted again the desire for some kind of united effort to face the difficult problems posed for congregations, and at the same time bring the Baptists into a larger fellowship. Several associations passed resolutions favoring some kind of cooperative endeavor.

Well aware of the early abortive effort at statewide organization, the Cumberland Association, nevertheless, in 1832, called a meeting of messengers to find ways to invigorate the churches and secure their cooperation in extending the Baptist cause. A proposal to establish a state agency for domestic missionary purposes was adopted. The following year, at the Mill Creek Baptist Church in Nashville, the Tennessee Baptist Convention was organized, a constitution adopted, and an executive committee of thirty members was authorized.

Scarcely was the convention devised before it was assailed from all quarters. Many Baptists, regarding with suspicion anything which tended toward centralization of authority and threatened local autonomy, looked upon the new instrument with dire misgivings. The structure had to struggle hard to weather storms of opposition and criticism hurled against it by Primitive Baptists, Gospel Mission Baptists, and other similar Baptist groups. Only through the diligent efforts of Robert B.C. Howell, a gifted Virginian who arrived in 1835 to reestablish the First Baptist Church in Nashville following the earlier defection of the original congregation to Alexander Campbell's restoration movement, did it survive. During his first year in Nashville, Howell became moderator and started publication of *The Baptist,* which he used primarily to inform churches about the work of the new agency. Through the columns of the paper news was carried to the churches of statewide Baptist activities, doctrinal issues were discussed, needs presented, and projects advanced.

The organization developed in influence and support increased, but it continued to be hounded by opposition. Much opposition evaporated, however, through one small act. It turned out that many opposed the structure simply because of the name itself. "Convention" was a new and unfamiliar term, creating suspicion among the conservative element. "Association," on the other hand, was acceptable Baptist terminology. An increasing number felt a simple change in the name, without altering its nature, would lead some who had opposed the convention to support it. In 1842, again at Mill Creek Baptist Church, its birthplace, the Tennessee State Convention was dissolved and the General Association of Tennessee Baptists succeeded it.

The General Association was slightly different from the organization it replaced. Four societies which had been auxillary to the convention were merged into it, and five boards were established. It was specified also that the purpose of the association was to aid feeble and destitute churches, to provide missionary programs to both home and foreign lands, and to supply religious literature to members. Because of the geographical barriers separating the state into three divisions and the difficulty of east-west communication, there never really existed a comprehensive state organization. Instead, from 1842 to 1874, there were three sectional associations: the Middle Tennessee Association of Baptists, the East Tennessee General Association of Baptists, and the West Tennessee

Convention of Baptists. The statewide General Association failed to unite all of the churches into a strong cooperative body, and the matter of boards, conventions, and associations remained a divisive issue among Baptists as Missionary Baptists, Gospel Mission Baptists, and Primitive Baptists arrayed against one another in constant debate.

The Christian Church (Disciples of Christ), with roots both in the Presbyterian and Baptist denominations, evolved into an organizational structure quite similar to that of the Baptist. Congregations in the Nashville area, around 1842, began working in unison through a "cooperative" to promote and sustain evangelistic enterprises. Careful not to jeopardize the principle of local church autonomy, cooperatives were gradually organized at district and state levels. The affairs of the cooperatives, at each level, expanded beyond evangelistic concerns and were handled at annual meetings. District cooperatives also became almost identical to Baptist associations; the state cooperatives resembled the Baptist general associations. Because of conditioning through cooperative endeavors, members of the Christian Church in Tennessee became willing participants when the movement organized nationally in 1849.

The five evangelical bodies maturing denominationally during the three decades before the Civil War were joined during the period by two already highly structured denominations, the Episcopal and the Lutheran.

A heritage of enmity, resulting from an identification of the Episcopal church with England during the American Revolution, delayed the Episcopalians in getting established in the state. The introduction of the Episcopal church in Tennessee was the work of a Virginian who first ventured into the Cumberland region in 1821 to teach at Harpeth Academy at Franklin. But James Otey, feeling that he was looked upon with contempt, if not disgust, because of his church affiliation, returned to his home after one year of teaching. He had an affection for Tennessee, however, and after preparing for the priesthood, he again moved, in 1825, to Franklin, opened a school, and, in a more favorable environment, began holding Episcopal services in the Masonic Hall. In 1827, he organized St. Paul's Episcopal Church, the first Episcopal church in the state. Otey also organized St. Peter's at Columbia and began holding services in Nashville that led to the formation of Christ Church in 1829. On July 1, 1829, with three clergymen and representatives from the three congregations meeting in the Masonic Hall in Nashville, the Episcopal Bishop of North Carolina led in the formation of the Diocese of Tennessee.

The Episcopal Church grew slowly, gaining communicants only in

towns and cities and among prosperous land owners. In 1834, when Otey became the first bishop of the diocese, there were only 11 churches and 9 clergymen. Christ Church had 34 communicants; St. Paul's 23. On the eve of the Civil War, there were only 26 parishes containing 1,506 communicants.

While Lutheranism appeared early in Tennessee and there was a congregation in Sullivan County at the beginning of the nineteenth century, it was not until 1820 that the Synod of Tennessee was established. The first Lutheran church in Middle Tennessee, organized in 1823, was located on the Duck River near Shelbyville. Dependent more on German migration than on settled residents, the denomination grew slowly. The number of ministers never equaled the demand and many Lutherans united with other denominations. In 1850 there were but twelve congregations in the state, mainly in East Tennessee; only six new ones were established during the next decade.

Two religious groups beyond the pale of Protestantism also appeared. Roman Catholicism and Judaism had inauspicious beginnings, however, and never threatened the Protestant domination of the state.

Roman Catholic priests traveled into Tennessee from Kentucky on church missions during the early nineteenth century. One of these, the Reverend Stephen Badin, visited the scattered Catholics four times between 1808 and 1810 and was encouraged by the prospects for establishing Catholic parishes in the state, especially at Knoxville and Nashville. It was a decade before a second missionary, the Reverend Robert Abell, entered the state and in May 1821 held formal masses for Nashville Catholics. In 1826 a Bardstown seminary professor wrote that the few Catholics in the state were visited two times a year by a priest and that a building in Nashville, erected for use as a Catholic church, served as a schoolhouse for Protestants. It was not until 1830 that a parish was formed in Nashville, the first in the state.

By 1837 several parishes had been established and the Diocese of Nashville—which included the entire state—was organized. The Right Reverend Richard Pius Miles, a native of Maryland, was consecrated as the diocese's first bishop. Bishop Miles, an indefatigable missionary, was largely responsible for the formation of new parishes. It was not long before he had thoroughly organized his diocese, launched a seminary and a school for boys, gathered around him a number of capable

James Otey, first Episcopal bishop.

nuns and priests, established an orphan's home and a hospital, and built a cathedral, later to be called St. Mary's. The growth of Roman Catholicism became especially noticeable when a large number of Irish moved into the state around mid-century to work at bridge and railroad construction. Moving mainly into the Chattanooga, Memphis, and Nashville areas, the new residents not only increased the size of established parishes, but became the nucleus for new ones. Unfortunately, the growth of Roman Catholicism elicited a barrage of insults and slander from a segment of the Protestant press, pulpit, and membership. Fortunately for Roman Catholicism, Bishop Miles, a man of wisdom, patience, and education, maintained his dignity in the midst of the intolerant attacks and won the confidence and friendship of many broad-minded Protestants as he continued to extend Catholicism.

While there were Jews in East Tennessee as early as 1790, and in Middle and West Tennessee by 1840, organized Judaism appeared late. At the outbreak of the Civil War, there were only two synagogues in the state, one in Nashville and the other in Memphis. In 1851 the Orthodox Jews in Nashville organized a benevolent society and rented a room near the present Louisville and Nashville railroad depot for use as a meeting center. Two years later, after the arrival of Rabbi Alexander Iser, a Russian Pole, the society reorganized as a synagogue and adopted the name "Kahal Hakodesh Mogen David," which meant the "Holy Congregation — the Shield of David." A similar organizational path was followed in Memphis, where, by 1850, there were enough Orthodox Jews to organize a benevolent society which, also in 1853, became a worshiping synagogue under the name "B'nai Israel Congregation Children of Israel." Ideological conflict developed almost at once between those who supported extreme orthodoxy and those who favored moderate reform. The conflict began to resolve itself, and, by 1860, the congregation inclined in the direction of reform. It was not until 1862 that a Reform congregation was established in Nashville.

In addition to ecclesiastical organizations among the Protestant denominations, religious periodicals also contributed to identification and relationship with a denomination beyond the local level. In reaching the membership, the denominational press, next to the pulpit, was the most important instrument in each of the denominations in promoting specific doctrines and practices while minimizing and combating those of the competition. The journals, normally the endeavor of an individual, began to appear after 1830; within a short time each denomination had its organ through which enterprises were advocated and triumphs made known. Reports from various congregations and activities by church leaders were found in nearly every issue of a periodical, serving to make the reader aware of what was taking place beyond the local congregation. Whether published officially by a specific denomination or privately in the interest of a particular denomination, through the pages of these publications some people learned for the first time that there were others beyond their area committed to the same religious objectives and principles that they held. The printed page welded the scattered congregations into a communion as nothing else was able to do.

As might be expected, the first religious papers were established by the Presbyterians. In 1826 the *Calvinistic Magazine,* published at Rogersville, began circulating in the Synod of Tennessee. It ceased publication after four years but was revived in 1845. When it and a successor failed because of inadequate financial support, the *Christian Observer,* published in Richmond, Virginia, became the denominational organ for Tennessee Presbyterians. The Cumberland Presbyterians began the *Revivalist* in 1832 at Nashville. It remained the official publication of the denomination until 1840, when it ceased publication. After that, the Cumberland Presbyterians had no official publication until 1874, but there were several private journals printed in the interest of the denomination.

Among the Methodists, religious journals gave the denomination an instrument for communication in each of the conferences. In the Tennessee Conference it was primarily the *Nashville Christian Advocate;* in the Holston Conference it was the *Holston Christian Advocate;* and for West Tennessee Methodists it was the *Memphis Christian Advocate.* These three merged in 1854, with the *Nashville Christian Advocate* the surviving journal to serve the total state interest of the denomination.

In 1835, Robert Howell began *The Baptist* in Nashville and it was soon considered the vehicle for Tennessee Baptists. Because of financial difficulty, the paper ceased publication in 1839. Publication was resumed in 1844. Three years later the name was changed to the *Tennessee Baptist* and the editorship passed from Howell to James R. Graves.

The first journal of the Christian Church was published in Paris in 1836, but it ceased publication after a year, and it was not until 1844 that another paper, the *Christian Review* began publication in Nashville. The *Review* and a successor ceased publication in 1853. Afterward, Tolbert Fanning and William Lipscomb began the *Gospel Advocate.*

The editors of the various publications were usually good writers and reporters. Conversant in doctrinal standards of their denominations, they functioned as moderately competent theologians. Generally well-respected and considered denominational leaders, the editors, in articles and editorials, did not hesitate to express personal views. In this respect, all of them appeared restrained when compared to James R. Graves, the controversial editor of the *Tennessee Baptist,* whose published sentiments kept the Baptists in a constant state of turmoil. As the ardent champion of "landmarkism" — a movement that placed extreme emphasis on congregational autonomy and on strict membership requirements — Graves, sowing discord and divisiveness, exerted a strongly conservative influence and became the most powerful leader among Tennessee Baptists, all the while eliciting probably more rebuttal, anger, frustration, and animosity than all the other religious editors combined.

Almost without exception the successful journals were based in Nashville. In addition to using the equipment to produce the periodicals, the presses published Bibles, books, tracts, and Sunday School literature. This activity rapidly made Nashville the religious publishing center of the state. When the Southern Baptists decided to locate the Southwestern Publishing House in Nashville, and the Methodists the Southern Methodist Publishing House, the capital city became the religious publication center of the South.

Some church leaders were attuned very early to the value of educational institutions in inculcating sound doctrine, facilitating membership expansion, and reinforcing denominationalism. Plans for and the actual founding of colleges were major factors in contributing to a sense of identification with a denomination. After 1830 there were intense efforts by evangelical Protestants to establish denominational colleges in the state and to use them as strategic agencies for building denominational identity and extending denominational views. Each denomination carefully nurtured and supported its schools, quickly placing most of its graduating young men into the service of the church. Annual reports were made on the number of ministers being trained, the numbers of "pious students" enrolled, and the spiritual state of the faculty.

Presbyterians, the earliest and virtually alone in giving attention to the education of ministers and members, had established colleges almost as readily as they had established churches. By 1800 there were two colleges in East Tennessee and the beginning of a third in Middle Tennessee. Samuel Doak had founded Washington College and Samuel Carrick had

---

James R. Graves, controversial editor and preacher, probably the best-known conservative Baptist during the nineteenth century.

founded Blount College. In Nashville, Thomas Craighead, the first resident Presbyterian minister, had opened Davidson Academy in 1786, which later became Davidson College. Eventually it merged with Cumberland College and that union took form as the University of Nashville. The first president of the new university was a Presbyterian clergyman, Philip Lindsley, who was destined to play a leading role in higher education.

Early in the nineteenth century, Hezekiah Balch founded Greeneville College, and Samuel Doak, along with his son John, established Tusculum Academy, later to become Tusculum College. Isaac Anderson, meanwhile, became interested in opening a theological seminary. He impressed the Synod of Tennessee with his idea, and in 1817 the synod made plans to establish the "Southern and Western Theological Seminary." The fledgling institution opened, with a class of five students, in Anderson's home in Maryville, near the Presbyterian church he served. The seminary flourished. At the end of a decade, ninety students were enrolled, taught by a faculty of four, supported in part by a modest endowment. But within a few years the institution began to decline as a school of theology and to assume the character of a college, until, in 1842, the name was changed to Maryville College. But the institution continued to provide instruction in theology until 1855.

Less active and less successful in founding educational institutions than the Presbyterians, the Cumberland Presbyterians, nevertheless, had developed enough organization and identity to participate in the wave of enthusiasm for establishing denominational colleges. They established two college level institutions in Tennessee during the period. With bright prospects for a sizeable student body and promise of financial support, Cumberland University was founded at Lebanon in 1842. With able leadership, the school was a success. Efforts were made to provide theological courses, and in 1846 the president, T.C. Anderson, and other Cumberland Presbyterian ministers delivered theological lectures to ministerial candidates. This proved unsatisfactory, and in 1854 a theological department was established. It did not experience the success that characterized the rest of the university; as late as 1860 it had only 2 professors, 9 regular students, and 11 "irregular" students.

Bethel College developed out of Bethel Seminary, established by the West Tennessee Synod in 1842 at McLemoresville. In 1847 plans were made to make the seminary a college, provided an endowment of $50,000 could be secured. The funds were not acquired, but the change was made anyway. In 1850 the first session of the college began, with an enrollment of about 150 students. In 1852 a theological department was added, and of the 165 enrolled in 1858, 15 were in that department. The Civil War closed the college, and when finally reestablished in 1872, it was located at McKenzie.

The Christian Church, in accord with its Presbyterian heritage, supported several colleges founded by Christian Church ministers. The first institution to which the denomination gave support was Franklin College, chartered in 1844 by Tolbert Fanning and located on the site of the present-day Nashville airport. To assist the Franklin College students in meeting expenses, Fanning had a unique idea: allow the boys who desired an education, but could not afford it financially, to perform manual labor in lieu of part of the fee. Students were allowed to work on Fanning's farm adjacent to the college to defray half of their expenses. The work program took the place of athletics. The success of Franklin College prompted the opening of a school for women, Minerva College, where the aim was to give "suitable facilities to girls for acquiring a Classical, Mathematical, and Scientific, as well as an ornamental education."

Another Christian Church institution was established on the top of the Cumberland Mountains at Spencer. Named for Elihu Burritt, an educated blacksmith whose writings on social and economic subjects enjoyed wide circulation in the state, Burritt College was chartered in 1848. Virtually cut off from all transportation and communication, the founder had selected the secluded location, determined that nothing should interfere with college work. After ten years, when the student body numbered about 200, a major crisis developed. The president, William Carnes, in an effort to prevent students from drinking expelled a number of the heavier drinkers and, simultaneously, attempted to get the sheriff to locate and destroy the stills in the mountains. All of this was detrimental to one of Van Buren County's main industries and pasttimes. Local feelings were aroused. Carnes's home was burned, and he resigned.

The Primitive Baptists fought education with such vigor that no effort on behalf of higher education among other Baptist bodies had a chance to succeed until around 1835. Spurred by competition — when made aware that the educated sons and daughters of wealthy Baptist members nearly all joined other denominations — and by the wave of college building, Baptists slowly responded to the strong pleas made by R.B.C. Howell and others for the establishment of colleges. Howell took the initiative when he proposed, in 1838, that the Baptists finance a theological department at the University of Nashville. Nothing came of the proposal, but in 1840 the Baptist Educational Society, organized in 1836, passed a resolution, at Howell's prodding, advocating the establishment of Union University somewhere in Middle Tennessee, with branches in the eastern and western parts of the state. Murfreesboro was chosen as the site, and classes began in 1841. As late as 1847 the school was only partially organized, with two professors and sixty students. Early in 1848 the institution moved to a new sixteen-acre campus, just out of town on the Woodbury Pike. When classes started in the fall there were approximately 150 students in all departments. The East and West Tennessee campuses, however, were never activated.

In 1850, Baptists in both the eastern and western parts of the state began educational enterprises on their own. The Mossy Creek Baptist Seminary, in Jefferson County, was chartered. In 1855 the seminary changed the name to Mossy Creek Baptist College, the forerunner of present-day Carson-Newman College. The college made progress, and by late 1859 it was able to report the receipt of "full patronage from the denomination." Meanwhile, Baptists in West Tennessee made plans to build a college near Jackson. The school was started, but because of difficulty in raising funds and securing students, it closed in 1861. The West Tennessee Baptists were more successful with a college established for women. A school formed in 1850 at Brownsville was well supported by the churches and continued for many years. Middle Tennessee also supported a college for women, Eaton Female College at Murfreesboro. Established in 1848 as the Female Institute, it changed its name in 1855 to perpetuate the memory of the founder, the Reverend Joseph Eaton.

The Methodists were initially prodded into educational ventures by Thomas Stringfield, an energetic East Tennessee minister. Deprived of any formal training, he became a champion of higher education and in 1825 was instrumental in getting the Holston Conference to consider the feasibility of establishing a conference-supported college. The study committee recommended the establishment of a college at Knoxville. When Holston Seminary opened in 1827, however, it was not in Knoxville, but in New Market. Ten years later its name was changed to Holston College. Holston Methodists were aggressive in providing educational opportunities for women. They established East Tennessee Female Institute at Knoxville and in 1857 began supporting Athens Female College, but the Civil War forced the closing of both.

Middle Tennessee Methodists co-operated with those in Alabama and Mississippi in establishing LaGrange College at LaGrange, Alabama, ten miles south of Muscle Shoals. When the school opened in 1830, seventy men enrolled. The size of the student body increased annually, but financial difficulties threatened the daily operation. With the promise of more adequate financing the college moved to Florence in 1855 and the name was changed to Florence Wesleyan College. After the Civil War the property was given to the State of Alabama and became the basis of present-day University of North Alabama. The middle area was especially aggressive in providing educational opportunities for women. During a period of five years, beginning in 1848, four institutions were founded — Clarksville Female Academy, Tennessee Female Institute at Columbia, Soule Female College at Murfreesboro, and Pulaski Female School.

The Episcopal church, nationally, gave almost total attention to the establishment of secondary academies and placed hardly any emphasis on founding colleges. Only a few institutions of college or university rank were ever founded permanently by the denomination, but one of these was in Tennessee. Bishop James Otey was one of the small number of leaders interested in founding a college. In 1837 he projected the establishment of Madison College in Tennessee, only to have the plans aborted by the serious economic depression of that year. Following years of preliminary discussion about a college for Episcopalians in the South, Leonidas Polk, bishop of Louisiana and former rector of St. Peter's Church in Columbia, made the proposal that the nine southern dioceses cooperate in establishing a school at a conveniently located site. A ten-thousand acre Sewanee mountain top tract was conveyed to the denomination, and in October 1860 Bishop Polk laid the cornerstone for the first building of the University of the South. With the growing bitterness between the North and the South, the name evoked accusations of sectionalism. The Civil War stopped construction. Bishop Polk did not live to lead in the completion of the project. A West Point graduate, he became a lieutenant general in the Confederate army and was killed at the battle of Pine Mountain, near Marietta, Georgia, in 1864. After the war, Bishop Charles Quintard, the second bishop of Tennessee and a former Confederate chaplain, assumed the responsibility for completing the institution and was present when the first session began in September 1868.

The maturing denominationalism — fostered through organization, journalism, and education — found opportunity for expression through pronouncements on important issues of the times. The several denominations spoke with differing levels of authority, and the individual congregations responded with varying degrees of enthusiasm. While the denominational statements of the Methodists and Presbyterians were the most authoritative, and those of the Baptist and Christian Church the least, the stated positions did represent collective judgment.

The catalog of immediate concerns included gambling, horse racing, card playing, theater attendance, Sunday mail, and dueling. But excessive consumption of alcoholic beverage, the use of tobacco, dancing, and secret societies were the main issues the Tennessee denomination addressed. These were seen as the most serious threats to church standards and became the major targets against which reforming zeal was directed.

The one great evil that probably exceeded all others in Tennessee was alcoholic intemperance. In many homes a supply of whiskey was considered as essential as sugar or salt. Some ministers engaged in the making and selling of whiskey. Even preaching services, weddings, and funerals were on occasion times for serving and drinking quantities of whiskey. Generally no social stigma was attached to drinking; only gross inebriation was frowned upon. But after 1830 there was a drastic lessening in the consumption of whiskey, and the decline was attributed largely to a concerted campaign against the use of the "tempting juice." Some ministers, however, appeared not to take the resolution seriously; in 1838 Baptist associations accused a number of Tennessee preachers of owning and operating highly profitable distilleries. The Presbyterians passed resolutions against the use of whiskey "except as a medicine," but the position of the denomination was not as positive as that of the Methodists and Baptists. The lack of a more definitive stance may have been due to the influence of ministers like Gideon Blackburn, who at one time sold whiskey wholesale and was able to collect from the federal government on a claim for liquor destroyed by Indians. After that, a man who heard Blackburn preach a temperance sermon remarked to several friends that "if any man ought to preach on temperance it ought to be Gideon Blackburn." The position of the Cumberland Presbyterians was firmer than that of the parent church, while the Christian Church staunchly opposed the sale and use of whiskey. The Episcopal denomination, meanwhile, adopted a position that allowed for the temperate use of intoxicants.

As in the use of ardent spirits, the Methodist church took the lead in denouncing the use of tobacco. The Cumberland Presbyterian and Christian churches joined the Methodist in taking strong stands opposing the use of the "filthy weed." The Baptists took little action against the use of tobacco and the Presbyterian position was quite mild.

Dancing and other amusements proved to be troublesome diversions from church activities, and the denominations were unwavering in their opposition to such past-times. A West Tennessee presbytery ruled that a dancer was guilty of "decidedly criminal" conduct and should be denied the privileges of the church. The other denominations endorsed this sentiment.

Secret fraternities, especially the Masonic Order, were seen as a rival religion and were regularly opposed. The secrecy that surrounded the order and an exposé by William Morgan, an alleged Mason, prompted the opposition. A leader in the Christian Church questioned whether a man ever became more spiritually inclined after he turned "to the ribbons, the apron, or the mystic symbols of a secret conclave." Church opposition, along with the exposé, led to the closing of most lodges in the small towns. The pressure was so strong in East Tennessee that by 1838 only two lodges were left intact.

As important as these issues were, they were overshadowed by one that dominated every interest in the state: black slavery.

There had been opposition to slavery from the time the first settlers moved into East Tennessee. Coming from states where slaveholding was firmly entrenched, they were well aware of the evils and injustices of the system. Slaveholding became a part of the scene, although there were comparatively fewer slaves in the state than in the remainder of the South. Since the frontier placed heavy emphasis on the rights of individuals, sentiment moved against human bondage. Of course, economic conditions also mitigated against slavery.

All three denominations active in Tennessee at the beginning of the century took a strong stand against slavery, declaring it contrary to the laws of God and harmful to society. The Baptists and Methodists, made up mostly of nonslaveholding whites, were especially adamant in their opposition. Seeing slaves as humans with souls precious in the sight of God, the two denominations, with their appeal to the poor, successfully evangelized among the blacks. Although segregated on church rosters and in worship services, blacks soon made up a sizeable percentage of church membership, frequently outnumbering whites in a particular congregation. As black membership increased, so did the sentiment for their freedom.

As the evils of slavery were increasingly discussed, and experienced, most ministers accelerated the intensity of their antislavery commitment. Clergymen took the lead in moving beyond the local congregation and organized antislavery societies. John Rankin, a Presbyterian, formed the first one, in Jefferson County in 1814. Within a short period there were societies in every East Tennessee county. These organizations, and a few others across the state, affiliated with a statewide organization, the Manumission Society of Tennessee, formed in 1815.

The strong antislavery sentiment that existed in East Tennessee led to the establishment, in Jonesboro, of the first newspaper in the United States whose avowed purpose was the abolition of black slavery. The *Manumission Intelligencer* was founded by Elihu Embree, a young Jonesboro businessman, in 1819 as a weekly publication. The next year it became a monthly publication and the name was changed to *The Emancipator*. After eight issues, Embree died, at the age of thirty-eight, and the publication ceased. But a similar journal soon replaced Embree's. In 1822 the Quaker Benjamin Lundy moved his year-old *The Genius of Universal Emancipation* from Ohio to Greeneville, where it remained until 1824, when Lundy moved to Baltimore.

But dramatically, the antislavery sentiment began to abate almost as quickly as it had developed. The primary reason was the fear of insurrection, fed by such incidents as the Nat Turner raid in Virginia in 1831. After that, many white ministers in the state who had championed antislavery views became more cautious in expressing themselves. Many saw black religion as a possible home base for revolution and backed away. In the retreat from moral opposition, ministers began to minimize the grander themes of salvation, justification, and regeneration and instead pronounced with mechanical regularity the importance of slaves obeying their master. Even the most ardent clerics committed to saving the souls of the blacks found themselves pressed to censor their sermons.

Joined with the fear of insurrection was the unbridled anger released at the militancy of the northern abolitionists, who, around 1830, pushed into Tennessee and assumed some of the functions of the more moderate antislavery societies. The seething resentment over "northern abolitionists meddling in the affairs of the societies and the state" was so pronounced that most local society leaders withdrew from antislavery activity, tolling the death of the movement. Within a very few years every antislavery society had entirely disappeared. In their place arose a determined defense of regional interests. The denominations, especially the Baptists and Methodists, reversing the Biblical injunction to transform and not conform, opted for accommodation with the status quo.

After retreating from earlier moral opposition to slavery, the churches began to defend the values of slavocracy. Aroused by the agitation of the ardent abolitionists, some clergymen even became apologists for slavery and, adjusting the gospel to the region, used Biblical passages to undergird their position. There were others, however, who, while defending the status quo, concluded that if slavery could not be ended, at least some effort ought to be made to convert the slaves to Christianity. They reasoned that by offering a religion containing the promise of a better life in the future, the churches could make the slaves' condition more bearable and that of the whites safer! The denominations began intensified programs to provide the slaves with religious instruction. This renewed concern for the disadvantaged carried over to the Indians also. Efforts to Christianize them had, as among the blacks, been going on for years but were now accelerated. Because the religionists sought to mold the Indians into the culture of the whites, the missionary endeavor was largely ineffectual. When the Indians were tragically removed from the state in 1838, over the "trail of tears," the missionary program ceased. But the evangelizing of the slaves was a different matter. Many were converted. The Baptists and Methodists, who still allowed emotionalism to be displayed lavishly at their services, captured the bulk of the converts.

The issue of slavery continued to be the pressing concern not only in Tennessee but across the nation. Facing the vexing question of the moral stance of the church, a somewhat moderate position of defense was taken in Tennessee, but in most of the other states extremists got unusual attention and gained control of national denominational activity. As dedicated northern abolitionists worked unceasingly to eliminate slavery, the southern apologists, equally opinionated, labored just as hard for its justification. Sectional differences became well marked as the controversy reached fever pitch.

Within the major religious bodies, denominational loyalties gave way to sectional interests and two separate parties emerged, headed for conflict. With the abolitionists on the move, southerners increasingly felt their way of life and worship threatened. More and more they began to feel that separation was the only means to preserve their faith and style of living.

The first schism occurred in the Presbyterian church in 1837. To the casual observer this was made to appear as primarily a division over a theological and practical argument, but slavery played a role. Since 1801 the Presbyterians and Congregationalists had cooperated, through a Plan of Union, to meet frontier religious needs, but at the 1837 General Assembly the Presbyterians elected to end the agreement because the plan had brought too many doctrinally lax Calvinists into the denomination. Many of those accused of lax Calvinism possessed antislavery sentiments; known as the "new school" section of the denomination, they were read out by the conservative "old school" group. The Synod of Tennessee identified with the new school, while the Synod of West Tennessee remained in the old school fold. In the new school the issue of slavery was debated constantly. Several strong resolutions condemning slavery were passed, and finally, in 1857, a split between the northern and southern branches of the new school took place. The Synod of Tennessee affiliated with the southern branch. By 1857 the Synod of West Tennessee had been divided into the Synod of Memphis and the Synod of Nashville. New school ministers who did not support the position of the new school were invited to affiliate with either of the synods. Only a few did.

The Baptist was the second of the major denominations to split over the slavery issue. Many northern Baptists, convinced of the sinfulness of slavery, questioned whether they could retain relations with southern Baptists who defended the institution. Agitation continued until the national meeting of Baptists in 1844. At that assembly, to test the good faith of the northern brothers, some southerners asked outright if the foreign mission board would appoint a slaveholder as missionary. The answer was no. From this point on relations between southern Baptists and the national structure grew more troubled. In the spring of 1845 enthusiastic delegates from eight southern states and the District of Columbia met in Augusta, Georgia, and organized the Southern Baptist Convention to carry on the benevolent and missionary work of the Baptist churches in the South. The act established a distinct Southern Baptist denomination which identified totally with the regional mores. Tennessee Baptists did not participate in the Augusta meeting, but immediately after the formation of the new body became enthusiastic supporters of it. When the Tennessee General Association met in October 1845, resolutions were passed highly approving of the organization of the convention. The 1851 assembly of the convention was held in Nashville.

Slavery also divided the Methodists. By 1836 many northern Methodist pastors were strongly abolitionist. They were equally matched by southern proslavery ministers. At the General Conference of 1836, the issue of slavery evoked a great deal of heat but no action. In 1840 a group of abolitionists broke away from the main body to form the Arminian Wesleyan Methodist church. Slavery was almost the only issue attended to by the General Conference of 1844. When that conference decisively upheld the suspension of a Maryland minister for refusing to free his slaves, southern Methodists knew the die was cast; division was inevitable. This breaking point came when Bishop James Andrew of

Georgia was ordered to cease his official duties until he freed the several slaves he had acquired through marriage. The bishop chose to fight the order. Southern delegates supported his stand. Tempers flared when the conference voted against Andrew. Then Bishop William Capers began work for a sectional division of the denomination. A plan of separation, detailing terms of division, was approved by the conference. In May of 1845, southern Methodists met in Louisville and, after voting over-whelmingly to separate formally, formed another body, the Methodist Episcopal Church, South. There were now two Methodisms. All of the conferences in Tennessee, reflecting the social and racial customs of the region, joined the southern branch.

The other denominations in Tennessee felt the effects of the issue of slavery but did not divide over it. The Christian Church took the posi-tion that slavery was not a matter of faith but of opinion, and with no national organization to rupture, the group rode out the storm. The Epis-copal church successfully held aloof from the controversy, but when the Protestant Episcopal Church in the Confederate States was formed in July 1861, effecting a separation, all of the southern states, including Tennessee, were found in the new body. Division did not threaten the conservative, democratic Cumberland Presbyterian denomination. Al-though its strength was in the South, and it held slavery to be a sin, a moderate leadership dominated.

Once the Tennessee denominations reached a definite position on the issue of slavery, there was an amazing acceleration of church activity. With most religious agencies — Sunday schools, missionary, Bible, tract, and temperance societies — stabilized, the denominations gave almost total attention to strengthening denominational lines. Busily engaged in sustaining themselves, the denominations enjoyed outward evidences of success — additions to membership, the erection of buildings, and in-creased social influence.

An ominous overcast, however, surrounded all of the activity. Most could see that the division of the denomination was prophetic of the po-litical division that was to follow. By 1860 crisis was at hand. In Decem-ber of that year, South Carolina seceded from the Union. Four months later Fort Sumter was shelled and the Civil War was on. It was a conflict destined to touch every family in Tennessee, and to create new problems for the churches.

4. Adversity and Adjustment

Hardly anyone failed to sense the tension sweeping the state. Many religious leaders, along with the rest of the people, saw the election of Abraham Lincoln as firm evidence that the Union of the thirty-four states would soon cease to exist. With the next occupant of the White House determined, South Carolina seceded, soon followed by five other southern states, and the cry went abroad that union, in reality, no longer existed and that Tennessee could not remain in the Union as it was then constituted. Some clerics joined the governor, Isham Harris, in advocating secession.

Tennesseans hesitated to secede. A referendum on the issue was announced. Clergymen took positions on either side, with the strongest voices against secession raised in East Tennessee. When the citizens had opportunity to express themselves on February 9, 1861, the majority voted not to sanction a convention that would have dealt with secession.

The vote greatly encouraged the supporters of union and motivated the opposition to increase the intensity of arguments for secession. By summer, secessionist sentiment was strongest in the center of the state and only a little less so in the west. The cause of the Union was strongest in the east. The most colorful and unique figure pleading for union was William G. Brownlow, ordained Methodist minister turned editor.

"Parson" Brownlow, whose partisan zeal and powerful resentments led his bishop to label him a "good hater," had been an itinerant minister in East Tennessee from 1826 to 1836. After 1836, he edited secular newspapers in Elizabethton, Jonesboro, and Knoxville. The editorship of the *Knoxville Whig,* in which he printed some of his most vehement diatribes, began in 1849 and continued until 1861. His attitude was set forth emphatically on the masthead of the *Whig: Neutral is Nothing.* He remained an ordained minister, but his activities were predominantly secular. In fighting for the integrity of union, Brownlow, who had earlier embraced slavery because of his hatred of abolitionists, had no peer.

Union sentiment in Tennessee, however, was not limited to the eastern portion of the state. In Memphis, Robert Grundy, minister of the Second Presbyterian Church, strongly opposed the disruption. The minister of the Second Presbyterian Church in Nashville, J.S. Hayes, was understood to be a Union man, as was a minority of his congregation. The Roman Catholic bishop of Nashville, James Whelen, expressed strong sympathy for the Union as did James Pendleton, pastor of the First Baptist Church and professor of theology at Union University in Murfreesboro.

Meanwhile, the secessionists were as active as the Unionists. Nowhere was there a sharper division of sentiment than in East Tennessee. In Knoxville, several clergymen favored joining the states that had withdrawn from the Union. One of them, William Harrison, minister of the First Presbyterian Church, and probably representative of an extreme position, "boasted in his pulpit that Jesus Christ was a *Southerner,* born on Southern soil, and so were his apostles, except Judas, whom he denominated a Northern man!" Harrison declared that "he would sooner have a Bible printed and bound in Hell, than one printed and bound north of Mason and Dixon's line!"

Verbal combat became outright war in April 1861, when shots were fired at Fort Sumter in Charleston harbor. Lincoln declared that the states which had seceded were in a state of rebellion against the United States and called for 75,000 troops to deal with the seceding states. The summons for troops, including some from Tennessee, led former Unionists to favor secession.

With sentiment running high in favor of Tennessee joining the Confederacy, a second referendum was held in June. The vote for secession carried by a margin of better than 2-to-1. On July 2, Tennessee, the last state to secede, became a part of the Confederate States of America. East Tennessee, where the vote had been more than 2-to-1 against secession, petitioned the legislature for the right to form a separate state. This was denied, but that portion of the state kept its representatives in the United States Congress through 1863.

Brownlow, convinced it was primarily the agitation of Protestant ministers and not the shelling of Fort Sumter or Lincoln's call for soldiers that had triggered secession, leveled one of his scathing blasts of censure: "I bring the charge of political preaching and praying against . . . clergymen . . . irrespective of sects; and I have no hesitance in saying . . . that the worst class of men who make tracks upon Southern soil are Methodist, Presbyterian, Baptist, and Episcopal clergymen, and at

the head of these for mischief are the Southern Methodists. I mean to say that there are honorable exceptions in all these churches; but the moral mania for secession had been almost universally prevalent among the members of the sacred profession."

War found its way inevitably to the state. With 775 battles and skirmishes fought on Tennessee soil, more than in any other state except Virginia, the conflict almost completely occupied the life and efforts of Tennesseans for four years.

Middle Tennessee was the first section of the state to bear the brunt. When Fort Henry on the Tennessee River and Fort Donelson on the Cumberland fell in quick succession in early 1862, Nashville was doomed strategically. On Sunday, February 23, 1862, the capital was formally occupied by Federal troops, the first major southern city to be captured. As Confederate forces abandoned nearly all of Middle Tennessee, Federal soldiers moved into the void. West Tennessee, meanwhile, was left open to invasion after the Confederate defeat at Shiloh. On June 6, Memphis surrendered, and before the end of July, Middle and West Tennessee were under Federal control.

The congregations of all communions were deeply affected by the armed conflict and the presence of Federal occupying forces. In the rural areas and small towns, many congregations could not hold services. In most instances this was because the edifices had been taken over for use as hospitals or barracks, or deliberately burned. Sometimes it was the result of members moving away, leaving too few to continue church activities. Some congregations that ceased to function were never reorganized. The Methodists and Baptists each lost approximately one-third of their membership during the course of the war.

As a general rule, when church buildings were left undisturbed there were services in them on Sunday. Some congregations, with no building in which to worship, met in private homes, stores, or wherever shelter could be found. The worshiping congregations, however, were made up mainly of women, children, and old men. The able-bodied men were at war. The minister of the Christian Church in Paris commented: "During the 4 years of the Civil War the meeting was kept up mainly by a few devoted sisters and two or three brethren."

"Parson" William G. Brownlow, ordained Methodist minister, who attained fame as the state's governor during Reconstruction. Original painting in the Tennessee State Library and Archives.

Denominational activities almost ceased. There were very few meetings beyond those of the local congregations: district, regional, and state assemblies were difficult, if not impossible. The Tennessee conference of the Methodist Church did not meet during the conflict, neither did the state organizations of the Baptist and Christian denominations. Denominational colleges closed, most of them taken over for use by the occupying army. Publishing enterprises came to a halt. In Nashville, the Methodist printing plant was seized for use by the United States government.

Nashville's religious life was severely restricted, primarily by the policies of the resident military governor, Andrew Johnson, whose administration made him the most "cordially despised" man in the city. Early in his administration, Johnson demanded an oath of allegiance to the Federal government from the community leaders, including the clergy. Only four clergymen ever signed the oath. But clergymen who remained in Nashville and pursued ministerial roles were under the watchful eye of the governor, even to the extent that sermons were censored.

War's wrath seemed vented on the churches, as nearly every congregation was forced into a period of neglect and practically every church structure in Nashville was taken over by Federal authorities. Some buildings which obstructed military plans were destroyed completely. Among those left standing, most — including First Baptist, First Presbyterian, and McKendree Methodist — were used as hospitals. Others were used as barracks. A few were used as administrative buildings. A number, including Second Presbyterian and Woodland Presbyterian, served as chapels for Federal troops. Several were used as stables, and Hobson's Chapel Methodist Church was commandeered as a storage house for army supplies. Once an edifice was taken over, former members of the congregation were denied any use of the facility. There is the melancholy example of young Francis McNairy, killed in battle, who lay unburied in his home for days because authorities refused the pleas of his mother to be granted the use of the First Presbyterian Church for his funeral.

Memphis fared better than Nashville. Although many obstacles were thrown in the way of religious activities in the Bluff City, and there was a marked decline in membership and attendance, there was no wholesale confiscation of church property. The only structure initially taken over by the Federal forces was Second Presbyterian Church. The building, with a seating capacity of 1,000, was used as a chapel for Union soldiers. Second Presbyterian was allegedly selected as reprisal for a resolution offering the "church bells to the Confederate army to be melted down for cannon." In 1864, former members petitioned President Lincoln for return of the edifice. Lincoln informed the military commander that the "United States Government must not undertake to run the church" and if there was "no military need for the church building" return it. With these instructions, the Union chapel ceased to exist and the building was returned to the congregation. Following the battles of Shiloh and Corinth in 1862, General Grant had "military need" of the First Baptist Church and Chelsea Street Presbyterian Church for use as hospitals. There was also "military need" of Linden Street Christian Church for use as a barracks, and First Cumberland Presbyterian Church, the largest Protestant church building in the state, for use as a hospital, barracks, and stables. Few other edifices and parsonages were disturbed in Memphis.

But it was in East Tennessee, where a deep division of sentiment existed, that conditions were the most perplexing. Both the Federal and Confederate armies traversed almost the entire length of the region four times, and the controlling force of the moment largely determined church activities.

Early military action favored the Confederates. Confederate supporters, with deep loyalties and fervid intolerance, seemed determined that Unionists and Confederates should not live together. Union sympathizers began to feel the heavy hand of the majority. With reason obscured by overstrained emotion, congregations and church leaders began to deal most uncharitably with those who expressed or displayed Union sympathies.

Baptists, Presbyterians, and Christian Church Unionists experienced reprisal, but only moderately so when compared to the Methodists. Almost the entire session of the Holston Conference on October 15, 1862, dealt with charges against ministers who were allegedly disloyal to the Confederacy. Disciplinary action was brought against a considerable number. After trials, several were expelled or suspended from the ministry; others were placed on probation. The tide of suspicion had not subsided when the next conference was held. In a ruthless abuse of power, additional clergymen were expelled and several suspended for specific periods. W.H. Duggan, an elderly cleric, was suspended because he had prayed for the Union. Another aged minister, James Cummings, even after being acquitted of charges, became a victim of harassment and intimidation and was forced to flee the state.

Then, in late 1863, the situation was reversed. In September, General Ambrose Burnside's Federal forces began an uneasy occupation. When Confederate General James Longstreet later departed upper East Tennessee, never seriously threatening the region again, the Unionists were in undisputed control and Confederate sympathizers began to receive some of the same type of treatment they had earlier disbursed. The resentful and intolerant acts of disciplining those who had refused to give allegiance to the Confederacy became a ghastly boomerang.

With Federal troops everywhere, many preachers with Confederate loyalty were forced to flee and their congregations were left distraught and confused. Those who remained paid a price. John Wright, a Christian Church minister who supported the Confederacy, was driven from his home for "27 nights in succession." He was frequently robbed and often the target of surprise attacks as he traveled. J.H. Martin and W.H. Harrison, Presbyterian ministers in Knoxville, were imprisoned for their outspoken support of the Confederacy. Following the battles of Chickamauga and Lookout Mountain, in the fall of 1863, most ministers, objects of fervid intolerance, were forced to flee Chattanooga to escape capture.

The fire of persecution, however, burned most fiercely among the Methodists. Because they were preachers in the Methodist Episcopal Church, South, Carroll Long and J.G. Swisher were seized by a mob as they traveled near Athens and were forced to carry a pole on their shoulders amid the jaunts and jeers of the crowd. Swisher, who was sixty-two years of age, died a few months later. About the same time, Jack Baillhart, an elderly preacher, was seized by a mob near Athens and made to ride on a rail, without a saddle. There were numerous reports of ministers being taken from their horses, "beaten into insensibility," and left alone in the woods. These revengeful acts even continued for several years after the war.

The leader in seeking retribution for earlier acts of reprisal was Parson Brownlow. Brownlow—who had suspended publication of his paper in 1861 but had been reestablished in the newspaper business by Federal leaders who correctly recognized the propaganda power of the zealous parson's editorial pen—had become infuriated by the actions of the Holston Conference in expelling Unionist clergymen. After the occupation of Knoxville by General Burnside, the first issue of the new *Whig* contained a blistering attack on the "rebel church." Brownlow never relented.

With occupying military units positioned across the state, and congregations struggling to accommodate to their presence, several northern denominational leaders began to look upon the state as a fertile field for missionary activity. Through letters written by Union army chaplains and other soldiers to friends, clergymen, and religious newspapers, denominational officials became aware of the existence of empty church buildings and also of edifices with only partial congregations, scattered throughout the state. Plans were made to send missionaries into the state, use the sanctuaries, and promote denominational programs. When it was discovered that these activities could be undertaken if the denominations secured government approval, the Methodist Episcopal church made the first move.

Bishop Matthew Simpson, ministerial colleague of Parson Brownlow, used his influence in Washington to get an order from Secretary of War Edwin Stanton placing "all houses of worship belonging to the Methodist Episcopal Church, South, in which a loyal preacher appointed by a loyal bishop does not now officiate," at the disposal of the northern branch of Methodism. The wording of the order was such that no building in the possession of the southern branch of Methodism was secure. Further, Stanton's order directed the military commander to provide protection for the missionaries.

Missionaries came immediately. In addition to East Tennessee, they arrived in Memphis, Nashville, Murfreesboro, and Shelbyville. Bishop Simpson visited East Tennessee in January 1864 and, in concert with Parson Brownlow, urged the reestablishment of the Holston Conference of the Methodist Episcopal Church to exist in the same area as the Methodist Episcopal Church, South, so that loyal Methodists would no longer have to "live under the iron rule of the" southern Methodists. The conference was organized in June 1865 around a nucleus of forty East Tennessee preachers and six from other conferences, but attempts to get membership and clergy of the southern Methodist Church to join were only partially successful. Many buildings of congregations of the southern branch were seized, however, and in numerous instances the evicted membership had to meet in public halls, private dwellings, and groves. The animosity that developed between the two Methodisms was bitter, deep, and lasting.

Secretary Stanton issued a second order directing the military commander to secure and turn over to the American Baptist Home Mission Society all Baptist churches in the state "in which a loyal minister" did not officiate. Next the secretary directed the military commander to place at the disposal of the agent of the Board of Home Missions of the United Presbyterian Church all houses of worship in which a loyal minister of that denomination was not officiating. Baptist and Presbyterian missionaries came into the state but not in the numbers and with the aggressiveness of the Methodists, which left one Methodist minister to declare: "The old church sheltered under the grand old flag has come back to the south."

Some of the missionaries were successful in gathering a few followers, but overall they were not influential in building much sentiment for the Union, except in East Tennessee. They did, however, serve to increase the bitterness of the strife and place another barrier between North and South. The zeal that was manifested by the northern denominations in forcing themselves into the state was ill calculated to further either the cause of the Union or religion.

But all of the religious enterprises were not confined to the home front. There was considerable activity in the military forces, fostered primarily through the endeavors of chaplains. The vast majority of the Tennessee chaplains served with Confederate units. Of the more than 700 ministers who had service as Confederate chaplains, approximately 50 were Tennesseans. Responding to the challenge to combat the evil and vice associated with military life, chaplains came from every Christian denomination in Tennessee. Almost one-third of them were Methodist. The Presbyterians, including the Cumberlands, had the next largest representation. Despite their adherence to the principle of separation of church and state, the Baptists had representation. Predominantly young men, with an average age of twenty-eight, a considerable number of them became denominational leaders after the cessation of hostilities.

The military ministers shared the hard life of the soldiers — they ate the same rations, marched with the troops, slept on the ground, and sometimes even fought in battle. They ministered to the spiritual needs of the men on the battlefield, in the camp, and in the hospital. One reported: "The work is hard, there are privations to be endured, exposure and discomforts are encountered, the work of the chaplain is demanding and often discouraging but it is rewarding work."

The list of duties performed and the services rendered by the chaplains on behalf of the soldiers is impressive: they preached to the soldiers as often as circumstances permitted; counseled with them; conducted prayer meetings; organized choirs; led Bible classes; collected money from soldiers to purchase tracts, hymnbooks, and Bibles; distributed religious literature; established camp and post libraries; visited the sick and wounded, reading to them and writing letters for them to their loved ones; administered the sacraments; comforted the condemned; organized army churches; collected clothing and medical supplies for the men; performed services for those confined to stockades; and conducted funerals for the deceased. No respecter of persons, the Confederate chaplains ministered to the wounded, dying, and imprisoned Federal soldiers as if they were their own.

Chaplains, almost all Protestant, were evaluated mainly by their preaching. Soldiers spoke not of attending worship or participating in church services, but of "going to preaching." In their preaching, the chaplains, like most of the civilian ministers, frequently professed to see the hand of God in both military victories and defeats. Early Confederate victories were seen as evidence of God's favor. As the war was prolonged and victories were replaced by defeats, preachers labored the theme that God was punishing the South for its own good. Southerners had turned from God and relied too much on man. Repent, turn to God, and victory would result. As late as the spring of 1865, preachers, both military and civilian, were still urging people to repent of their sins of swearing, drinking, avarice, and licentiousness, lest God permit the Confederacy to fall.

Most of the chaplains gave primary attention to religious activities. But there were several who had too much interest in Caesar's affairs and imbibed in the spirit of war. Probably the most enthusiastic of these few was Thomas Caskey, for a time minister of Linden Street Christian Church in Memphis. Caskey carried a "Colt's rifle, double cylinder, eight charges for each, one of them in his gun, the other in his pocket, and two Navy sixes in his belt." He became known as the "fighting parson." Writing after the conflict, Caskey declared: "Apart from singing, praying, and preaching . . . taking care of the sick, comforting . . . the dying, and burying the dead, I would get pugnacious. The old Adam would overcome the new. I would shoulder a gun . . . I tried to break as many legs as I could. Had all done as I did . . . the number of artificial legs would have been greatly multiplied . . . I commend this mode of fighting." Fortunately for the cause of religion, there were not many like him.

Aware that there were not enough chaplains to minister adequately to the soldiers, most of the denominations devised plans for missionaries to supplement the work of the chaplaincy. Civilian ministers were urged to devote either part or all of their time, under the direction of the missionary societies of their denominations, to work among the soldiers.

Through the preaching of the chaplains and missionaries, revivals began in late 1862 among the soldiers in Tennessee and continued intermittently throughout the war. To hold converted soldiers firm in the faith, the preachers in the camps tried to organize army churches. When no churches were constituted, as a rule more informal organizations—

Christian associations—were formed. These organizations, consciously down-playing factionalism and sectarian differences, advanced an ecumenical spirit. Promulgating no creed except "redemption through Christ," the churches and associations sought the "reformation of swearers, and gamblers, the reclaiming of backsliders, and the building up of those who have become indifferent to the Master." Without these activities, religion would have played a rather subdued role in the regiments, posts, and hospitals.

With the surrender of General Lee at Appomattox on Palm Sunday, April 9, 1865, the period of Reconstruction replaced the Civil War. But for all practical purposes, reconstruction for Tennessee had begun in 1862. The last state to secede had been the first to succumb to the Union Army, and the appointment of Governor Andrew Johnson made him the first military governor of any state. A month before Lee's surrender, Parson Brownlow—after two earlier unsuccessful attempts—with a majority of the voters outside of East Tennessee disfranchised, had been elected governor. His inauguration marked the transfer from a military to a civil form of state government. Consequently, Reconstruction became a civil affair. Tennessee was one of the states of the old Confederacy to escape military reconstruction and the burden of a "carpet-bag" government. The Reconstruction period continued until 1870, when John C. Brown, a former Confederate major general and a Democrat, was elected governor by a large majority.

During civil Reconstruction, denominations focused attention on rebuilding sanctuaries that had been destroyed, repairing those that had been damaged, and repossessing those that had been seized. With members already financially burdened, most congregations filed claims with the federal government for aid, since the destruction and damage had resulted from federal misuse. The bureaucracy delayed action for years, and even when reimbursement was eventually made, it covered only a fraction of construction costs. Most of the rebuilding had to be funded locally, and it reflected the deep desire to reestablish normal religious activity.

Rebuilding proved burdensome, but the task was far easier than that of regaining buildings that had been seized by the military. President Lincoln, as early as 1863, had ordered the return of church structures to the rightful congregations unless the structures were absolutely necessary for military operations, but the order caused very few edifices to be vacated.

Displacing the northern denominations from the seized church buildings also proved difficult. Only infrequently did these bodies voluntarily terminate their tenancy. Instead, they chose to wait for eviction by the same government that had installed them. Again, difficulty was most evident among the Methodists. In Nashville, for example, trustees of McKendree Methodist Church, led by Parson Brownlow, declared they would not vacate the building until ejected by the federal government. Wiser counsel prevailed, however, and the change of occupancy was accomplished quietly. In East Tennessee, a southern Methodist cleric testified in late 1866 that over one hundred churches and several parsonages were being "illegally" held by the northern Methodists. When diplomacy and negotiations failed to get the property, lawsuits were filed. Controversy over property crippled both Methodisms, and it was not until around 1875 that the issue eventually was worked out by local congregations. But the bitterness between neighbors, who had been on opposing sides, continued to poison relations for years.

Regular meetings of conferences, conventions, associations, and presbyteries were resumed at war's end. Denominational activities were rekindled and rebuilding extended to church supported educational institutions and to religious publications. All of the denominational colleges had ceased operations during the course of the war. The Presbyterian, Cumberland Presbyterian, and Christian Church colleges, with difficulty, resumed classes. Among the Baptists and Methodists there were realignments. While the present Carson-Newman College had been firmly established by 1870, Union University at Murfreesboro was a different matter. Occupation of the property by Federal troops left the buildings in shambles. Although the school reopened in 1869, failure to secure financial support and students forced a permanent closing in 1873. When a statewide Baptist convention was formed in 1874, among its first acts was the approval of the establishment of a denominational college at Jackson, named the Southwestern Baptist University. The property of the Methodist school at Athens, Athens Female College, came into the possession of the northern Methodist church, but the distinctively local reputation of the school prompted several northern Methodist leaders to advocate a regional university. In 1873 Knoxville University, at first called Central Methodist University, was projected. For lack of support, Knoxville University was stillborn. Meanwhile, some southern Methodists talked of a regional university of their own. Under the leadership of Bishop Holland McTyeire, the institution was founded in 1873 and endowed by Commodore Cornelius Vanderbilt with a half-million dollar gift which he increased to a million dollars in 1876. Although many bishops and church members were suspicious of its probable impact, Vanderbilt University began almost immediately to exert an important influence on higher education in and beyond the state. The Presbyterians chartered King College at Bristol in 1868 and in 1873 began operating Southwestern Presbyterian University at Clarksville.

During the war, religious periodicals in Tennessee had ceased publication. Four of the five denominations which had periodicals before the conflict resumed publication during Reconstruction. Only the Presbyterians failed to reestablish a state-based religious journal. The Cumberland Presbyterians purchased several privately owned periodicals and consolidated them at Nashville into the *Banner of Peace.* Several new Baptist papers and publishing enterprises appeared. The *Gospel Advocate* was revived by Tolbert Fanning and David Lipscomb as the journal for the Christian Church. It was not long before an influential and profitable publishing business developed around the *Advocate.* The *Christian Advocate* resumed publication in January 1866, and the Methodist Publishing House grew steadily into a position of national promise, mostly through the strong drive and influence of Holland McTyeire and John McFerrin, the two best-known Methodists in Middle Tennessee. By 1880, printing and publishing had become the leading industry in Nashville, and much of this activity centered around religious publications.

As the congregations regained and rebuilt their physical facilities, they worked to reclaim membership and to add to it. Special efforts directed at the unchurched and those who had affiliated with northern denominations produced a revival movement almost equal to the one at the beginning of the century. The five leading evangelical bodies shared in the movement, but the southern Methodists and Baptists were the most aggressive and competed intensely with each other for converts. In

---

Above left: First Cumberland Presbyterian Church, Memphis, the largest building in Tennessee during the Civil War period. In addition to providing seats for a huge congregation, the church housed a mammoth pipe organ and had the state's first paid choir. *Above right:* When several denominations established publishing houses, Nashville became the religious publishing center of the South. Shown here is the Southern Methodist Publishing House. *Below:* Roger Williams University, on the site of present-day Peabody College, was one of several institutions founded in the state during Reconstruction to provide educational opportunities for blacks.

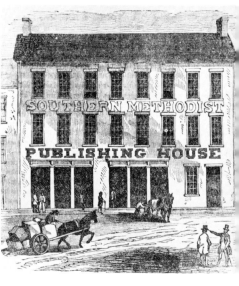

East Tennessee the southern Methodists not only had to contend with the southern Baptists but with the northern Methodists as well. Southern Methodist clerics, many of whom were descendants of those who had cut their pastoral teeth on quarrels with the Baptists, were not adept at dual assault. Because of this, the Baptists, who appeared to have gotten many of their perennial theological disputes settled, gained numerical leadership. In the five-year period that began in 1870, Baptist membership doubled, while the Methodist gain was only half of that. But the Baptist gains did not hold. About the time Reconstruction ended, there was a resurgence of "landmarkism." The renewed emphasis on extreme localism and exclusiveness developed enormous disruptive powers, and between 1876 and 1880 the Southern Baptist churches in Tennessee lost almost half of their membership, dropping from 101,241 to 57,090. Astoundingly, in 1880 the Southern Baptists, in terms of membership, were about where they had been in 1870.

The competition between the Baptists and Methodists for converts rekindled an intense sectarianism that extended into the other denominations. During the war, adversity had led the denominations to work cooperatively. Now the spirit of ecumenicity was cast aside and old animosities were redrudged. A residue of hostility surfaced. Baptist James R. Graves, who had moved his publishing enterprises to Memphis, led in a vituperative campaign against the Methodists. Diatribes that circulated as tracts and pamphlets several decades earlier were reissued and widely dispersed. Graves ridiculed the Methodist church as an "infant pseudochurch." At times he declared it to be no church at all, but "an anti-Christian organization," a miserable granddaughter of "the woman clothed in scarlet who put the saints to death." The Methodists replied vigorously, defending Methodism from slander and in turn slandering the Baptists. Methodists fired verbal blasts so frequently that their publishing house in Nashville was accused of burying the state in anti-Baptist tracts, periodicals, and books.

The intense sectarianism killed any chance that existed to unite the divided Baptist, Methodist, and Presbyterian denominations. Attempts at reunion served only to increase the sectarian spirit, especially when the northern wings attempted to dictate the terms. When this paternalism encountered the reassertion of sectarianism, reconciliation came to naught.

As noteworthy as the rebuilding and revival endeavors were, the most dramatic phenomenon during Reconstruction was the emergence of many exclusively black congregations and denominations. Prior to war, the blacks, both free and slave, attended church services along with the whites. There were fewer than ten exclusively black congregations in the state. Slaves were customarily members of the churches of their owners. They were seated in a segregated section of the church building, however, usually in the rear. Some people opposed "mixed services," but the practice was the rule. The slaves, who had no vote in the affairs of the congregation, were listed on the rolls as regular members, but were identified as blacks. While segregation was enforced in seating and in the administration of the sacraments, members, irrespective of color, "all sang and shouted together."

After Emancipation, and war's end, there was a radical change. To most blacks, freedom included doing things they had not been allowed to do before — riding horses, carrying guns, having names, and organizing. Rejoicing in their newly found freedom, they were not willing to worship in a church where they would be confined to certain sections, and where they were not counted genuine members. Free politically and socially, they wished to be free ecclesiastically. Blacks withdrew from the paternalistic, partially integrated congregations, chiefly in order to form their own churches and listen to their own ministers.

The largest number of the newly formed black congregations became affiliated with northern black denominations that had been founded earlier and moved into Tennessee during, and after, the war. The African Baptist Church, organized in Philadelphia out of a white congregation in 1809; the African Methodist Episcopal Church, also organized in Philadelphia in 1816; the African Methodist Episcopal Church, Zion, organized in New York in 1820 — all succeeded in getting black congregations to establish affiliation. Initially the two Methodist bodies were more successful than the African Baptist church, primarily because southern Methodist preachers encouraged the blacks to enter one of the African denominations. To reduce the likelihood of those who had been members of southern Methodist congregations from wandering into the white northern Methodist denominations, the white clergymen often went to elaborate lengths to transfer their black membership into either the African Methodist Episcopal Church or the African Methodist Episcopal Church, Zion. By 1863 each of these denominations had sufficient membership to organize a conference in Tennessee.

The southern Methodists, Baptists, Cumberland Presbyterians, and Christian churches all saw the trend of events and were quick to encourage the organization of independent black congregations and eventually denominations. Although many blacks were suspicious of the intentions of the southern churches, there was a generally favorable response. To save the "remnant of Black members," the southern Methodists encouraged the formation of separate congregations. By 1870, the black congregations had increased sufficiently to organize, at Jackson, the Colored Methodist Episcopal Church of America. The denomination grew rapidly and soon had two conferences and a publishing house at Memphis.

The largest portion of blacks, however, was attracted not by the Methodists but by the Baptist churches. Religious freedom which had meant so much to the growth of Baptists now became the main cause for expansion among blacks. Southern Baptists encouraged the formation of separate Baptist congregations, which were considered adjuncts to the associations in which they were located, and also to the state convention when it was formed in 1874. The white Primitive Baptist denomination, going counter to the Southern Baptist position, in 1865, at Columbia, organized a separate denomination for black members, the Negro Primitive Baptist Church. This, along with the other Baptist and Methodist bodies, accounted for approximately 85 percent of the black church membership in Tennessee.

The Cumberland Presbyterians in 1869, after aiding in the establishment of black congregations, assisted in the organization of the Colored Cumberland Presbyterian Church. The regular Presbyterian church in Tennessee repeatedly rejected attempts to form the several black congregations into a separate presbytery, and they functioned as part of the existing church structure. Christian Church members assisted in the formation of over a dozen black congregations in the state, mainly in Middle Tennessee. In 1867 these congregations were structured denominationally.

The only denomination in Tennessee that made a strenuous effort to run counter to the trend and accommodate blacks and whites in the same religious body was the Methodist Episcopal church. The denomination, with almost all of its membership in the Holston Conference in East Tennessee, vigorously courted black ministers and members. But in congregations where there was racial mixture, an uneasiness existed and a few unpleasant incidents were reported. And when the denomination began to lose white members, local congregations became less and less integrated. For all of the effort and controversy, less than 10 percent of the northern Methodist membership in Tennessee was black.

While the Methodist Episcopal church and other northern denominations did not win many blacks to church membership, they were determined to help them improve their circumstances. Attention was focused on providing educational opportunities. These efforts were marked with success.

The Congregational church, basically a New England denomination with hardly any congregations in Tennessee, was among the first of the denominations particularly active in educational endeavors. Interested more in the spiritual, intellectual, and moral uplift of blacks than in winning members, the Congregationalists did the lion's share of starting schools for blacks. Through the American Missionary Society, they opened Fisk University, first called Fisk School, in 1866 in an abandoned government building. By 1880 Fisk had acquired creditable status as an institution of college rank. Four years after starting Fisk, the American Missionary Society established Lemoyne Normal and Commercial School at Memphis, and the press periodically urged citizens to give it support.

The Methodist Episcopal church, through its Freedmen's Aid Society, opened Central Tennessee College in the unplastered basement of a black church in Nashville in 1866. The society quickly secured for its use an abandoned Confederate gun factory, but the factory was soon vacated in favor of a new building. The term "college" was an exaggeration, however. When it was indicted for being no more a college "than an egg is like a full-size rooster," serious efforts were made at improvement. In 1874 a bold step was taken when a medical department was formed. Named in honor of the Meharry family, which supported it financially, it was the first and only department for black medical students in the Mississippi Valley. Meanwhile, Tennessee Wesleyan College, the northern Methodist church school in East Tennessee, began admitting blacks.

The northern Baptists, through their Home Mission Society, began the Normal and Theological Institute at Nashville to train teachers and ministers for the Baptists. A surplus government building was moved to a lot near Fort Gillem, at the southwest corner of Polk and Park streets, and classes began in August 1867. After seven years, the school relocated to the site of present-day Peabody College. In 1883 the school became Roger Williams University. In 1910 a major portion of the property was purchased for Peabody College and proceeds from the sale were used to construct a new Roger Williams campus on Whites Creek Pike. The school moved to Memphis in 1928 and merged with Howe Junior College. The surviving institution became Roger Williams College.

The Presbyterian Church, U.S.A. concentrated its efforts on one institution in the South for blacks, and in 1872 started Knoxville College.

From the first, the institution was blessed with capable leadership. Because of adequate financial support, the school had good facilities, a qualified staff, and a growing student body. Established primarily to train blacks for the Presbyterian ministry, the nature of the school gradually changed. The process began in 1880 when black residents who were admitted received tuition grants from the state. Ten years later, for all practical purposes, the school became a branch of the University of Tennessee. To meet the requirement of equal facilities for all races and qualify for additional funds for land-grant colleges authorized by the Second Morrill Act — passed by the Congress in 1890 — officials at the segregated university arranged with the trustees of Knoxville College for that institution to "serve as the University's colored branch, receiving a proportionate share of the land-grant funds." This arrangement continued in force until 1909, when a legislative act established the Tennessee Agricultural and Industrial Institute near Nashville. Reverting to total control by the Presbyterians, the school, solidly established and supported, continued a distinguished record of service as a liberal arts college.

When blacks had meager resources and Tennessee whites were unable to accomplish much in their behalf, the black denominations and educational institutions had a major role in guiding them, against great odds, from a condition of slavery to an experience of freedom. Without the benefits of these organizations their upward social mobility would have been nearly impossible.

The evangelical Protestantism — reaching out almost exclusively to the salvation of souls, with ministry understood individualistically — that was reforged by competitive evangelism and regular congregational preaching, in the sectarian atmosphere of this period, set the pattern for religious activity in Tennessee for the remainder of the century, and for much of the next. With little sense of remorse for past evils and virtually devoid of social ethics, this type of religion was destined to be defensive of regional mores as it urged the self-conscious society to turn in upon itself. Playing a major role in conserving "the old ways," evangelical Protestantism became a powerful force and made a near conquest of the state's population. A few Roman Catholic and Jewish congregations were scattered across the state, mainly in the urban areas, but Tennessee had been Protestant from the beginning and was to remain so. And it was to be a distinctive Protestantism — individualistic, provincial, and unsophisticatedly directed.

5. Beyond the Sanctuary

As the nineteenth century ended and the twentieth got underway, there was extensive religious activity across the state in both accustomed and unaccustomed arenas. Protestantism was dominant, daily increasing its strength, impinging more and more upon the lives of the people. Religious enthusiasm gradually moved beyond concern for the salvation of the individual and the "spirituality of the church" to involvement in social issues, even to unprecedented intrusion into political affairs. It was watershed time!

Nowhere was the accustomed religious activity more evident than in membership development. Shortly before the beginning of the last quarter of the nineteenth century, over 279,664 persons — approximately 22 percent of the population — held membership in 3,178 different congregations. According to the religious census taken by the Census Bureau in 1906, over 697,570 individuals — 32 percent of the population — were counted as church members. While the population had increased by 72 percent, church affiliation had grown by almost 150 percent. Two groups, constituting three-fourths of all church members, added dramatically to their rolls: the Baptists, including the black churches, grew from 86,855 to 277,170 members; the Methodists, also including black congregations, increased their numbers from 117,832 to 241,396. Presbyterians, including the Cumberlands, moved from 48,928 to 79,337 members. The Christian Church at the beginning of the period had 17,784 members and in 1906, combined with the Churches of Christ, counted 56,315 members. These growing bodies accounted for almost 95 percent of those with church affiliation in the state. Additionally there were, in 1906, more than 17,000 Roman Catholics, primarily in the urban areas, over 7,800 Episcopalians, approximately 3,200 Lutherans, and almost 1,000 adherents of Judaism. Protestantism was still dominant.

The impressive increase in numbers came about as a consequence of the effort the churches instituted to build up local congregations. Again revivalism became the chief instrument for filling the pews, recruiting new members, and imparting vitality. Membership growth was measured by the ability of the churches to keep awake the revival spirit. The largest gain came when the revival spirit ran highest.

The revivals of these years were usually more restrained than those earlier in the century, but their influence was just as powerful and periodically the old manifestations were present. "Glorious revivals" were reported in place after place as the movement spread across the state year after year.

Baptists and Methodists gained much from revivalism, but no denomination participated more enthusiastically than the mainline Presbyterians. Denominational leaders had been made painfully aware that the Baptists and Methodists had greatly outstripped Presbyterians by using revivals to reach the rank and file of the people. Concerned that these bodies would dominate the future unless groups like the Presbyterians adapted to the imperative conditions for expansion, Presbyterians became very active participants in revivalism. It was not uncommon for excitement to run so high that services scheduled at Presbyterian churches for two weeks would be extended to three, occasionally to four weeks.

In connection with the revivals there developed a "holiness movement" among the Methodists which contained serious overtones. Methodism from its very beginning had placed strong emphasis upon the idea of Christian perfection, and shortly after the revival activity got underway a strong emphasis on this (sanctification) arose as people began talking of experiencing a "second blessing" or the "baptism of the Holy Spirit." In 1878 the Nashville *Christian Advocate* reported that interest in the "holiness movement" was statewide. "Venerable men are calling attention to it. Multitudes of awakened believers are seeking it. . . . The movement is the natural recoil of the religious mind from the rampant worldliness of the time." As the movement spread, its advocates grew; opposition developed just as strongly. Whole congregations were disrupted by disputes over sanctification, and agitation reached a high pitch during the eighties. "Second blessing pastors" appeared. Several Tennessee congregations divided over the issue, and occasionally parts of congregations broke off to form small independent fellowships. An estimated 3,000 Tennessee Methodists, strongly believing in sanctification, helped form the Church of the Nazarene, in 1894, by the union of eight holiness groups that had withdrawn from various denominations.

It was customary in most localities for the revivals to begin under the faithful preaching of the pastor. Gradually this practice gave way to a leadership provided by an imported minister. The trend prompted some clergymen to leave the local pastorate and become professional evangelists, moving from revival to revival, and "reporting only to God." In the towns and cities, Union Meetings, interdenominationally sponsored and conducted by professional evangelists, became common. In the large cities, the Union Meetings grew to be highly publicized major religious productions. In staging these, no city excelled Nashville, which seemed to have a monopoly on the services of Sam Jones, the most popular evangelist in the South.

When Sam Jones came to Nashville in 1885 to conduct his first Union Meeting, his reputation as a spellbinding sensationalist had preceded him. On the beginning May night, an immense crowd gathered in and around the large tent at the corner of Broadway and Eighth Avenue. Although Sam Jones "took his theology out of deep old wells with a Greek bucket and a Hebrew windless," he was never more effective than when he attacked the "liquor traffic." On the first night and every night that followed, Demon Rum became the object of his fiery verbal blasts. Jones frightened the congregations with the image of an omniscient judge, who gave out justice on Judgment Day, and he described the sentences for sinners in terms every sot could understand. From the midst of packed congregations, hundreds came down front to make the good confession. Among those who accepted Sam Jones wholeheartedly, because of his powerful sermons on the evils of whiskey, was a riverboat captain by the name of Thomas Green Ryman; his was a highly publicized conversion.

Ryman, who owned a fleet of steamboats that plied the Cumberland River, had considerable property along the Nashville waterfront. He had a bar on each of his steamboats, and, in a large waterfront building, Ryman operated a well-frequented saloon, the largest of the 170 in the city. After he "got religion," Ryman, under the watchful eyes of the press, went out to each of his boats, tossed the liquor overboard, and closed the bars forever. He had his saloon converted into a hall for religious and temperance meetings, and he called it the Sam Jones Hall. He also changed the name of his largest and finest steamer to the *Sam Jones*. So great was the magnetism of Jones and the affection for him, that many other converts, had they the means, undoubtedly would have responded as Captain Ryman.

The excitement, enthusiasm, and consequences that attended Jones' first Union Meeting brought him to Nashville for eighteen successive years of long preaching sessions, each a religious extravaganza. Immediately after his conversion, Ryman began to promote the construction of a tabernacle in which Jones could hold his revivals. Little was accomplished until Jones came to Nashville for his 1888 Union Meeting. At the conclusion of the final sermon in the series, $22,000 was raised to begin construction. When Jones arrived in town for his 1891 revival, a huge congregation had gathered at the Union Gospel Tabernacle to welcome him. From then on, when Jones delivered his emotion-packed sermons in Nashville, it was at the tabernacle. On December 25, 1904, at the conclusion of his remarks at the funeral of Captain Tom Ryman, Jones repeated a proposal made five years earlier; namely, that the name of the Union Gospel Tabernacle be changed to the Ryman Auditorium. His proposal was unanimously approved. The building carries this name to the present day.

One other popular revivalist, especially known for his city-wide campaigns, was B. Fay Mills. He devised a revival system which contained step-by-step instructions for advance preparations and the conduct of campaigns. It provided the model for meetings held in Memphis, Nashville, Knoxville, and other Tennessee cities.

In building up and strengthening the local congregations, revivals and regular worship were supplemented by several new local church organizations that involved men, women, and youth on a scale never previously attained.

Although the Sunday school had been a casual part of some church programs, it was only now that it received its most serious, systematic emphasis. The Baptists placed extraordinary stress on the Sunday school, seeing it as a strategic agency to bring people into contact with religious instruction, and then into church membership. Black Baptist congregations, as well as white, were urged to establish Sunday schools as part of the local church operation. And by 1881, the president of the State Convention of Colored Baptists was able to report a Sunday school in every church. When the Tennessee Baptist Convention was formed at Murfreesboro in 1874, the message to the assembly was that if the denomination were to continue its growth, attention had to be given

Union Gospel Tabernacle, Nashville, shortly after its completion in 1891. Later renamed the Ryman Auditorium — in honor of Captain Tom Ryman, popular owner of riverboats, who led in its construction — it was the scene of annual evangelistic campaigns conducted by the Reverend Sam Jones.

to enlisting members and prospects into regular, well-organized Sunday schools. Baptists aggressively promoted the schools by circular letters, institutes, and by individuals who went into congregations to assist in organization. The denomination was so successful that a Sunday School Board of the Southern Baptist Convention was established in Nashville in 1891. The Methodists kept pace. As the result of efficient leadership, publication of good literature, and tremendous promotional activity during the decade between 1880 and 1890, the denomination accelerated development from a very few churches with Sunday schools to the existence of more Sunday schools than congregations. In the other denominations, the emphasis on Sunday schools was almost as intense.

To develop Christian character in young people and to train them for Christian service, congregations made use of organizations designed especially for the youth. In the churches where Christian Endeavor Societies, Epworth Leagues, Methodist Young People's Organizations, and Baptist Young Peoples Unions were maintained, considerable numbers of young people were nurtured in wholesome Christian living. They were also trained for leadership in their own congregations. Through devotional services and work projects, the youth acquired a deeper understanding of the meaning of church life.

Responding to the opportunity to enlist women in special projects, churches began to organize and develop Women's Missionary Unions, Women's Home Missionary Societies, and Christian Women's Missionary Fellowships. Women, of course, had been involved in church activities from the beginning, in significant ways, but traditionally they were kept in the background. An indication of the increasingly active role of women in the church was seen in the emergence of the new agencies whose primary purpose was to provide support for home mission enterprises. To start new congregations, or assist struggling ones, the funds raised through the efforts of women were usually channeled into boards of church extension, another type of agency that appeared at this time. The success of Methodist women in Middle Tennessee in raising funds for distribution by the Board of Church Extension was credited with making the Tennessee conference the strongest conference in southern Methodism.

As the many church activities were carried out, problems and difficulties were encountered, but the obstacle considered most detrimental was "Sabbath desecration," or "Sunday breaking." The day was used too much for activities not associated with the church to suit many conservative Christians. Over the years the churches had been concerned with improper observances of Sunday, but misuse had become more prevalent, and more acceptable, in accord with the "spirit of the age." The growing laxity in regard to Sunday observance was traced back particularly to the Civil War, which knew no Sunday.

Alarmed at the inroads upon the traditional "Lord's Day," and its use as a day primarily for worship and rest, congregations exerted their influence to guard the sanctity of Sunday. Firm in the support of the traditional Puritan Sabbath concept, ministers called on members to respect the day and to "abstain from Sabbath desecration in its various forms, including social visiting, drives and excursions for pleasure, fishing and all kinds of worldly sport." When the Tennessee Centennial was held in 1897, nearly every Nashville congregation vigorously opposed any suggestion of Sunday openings. The outcry, however, was not heeded.

To insure a "Lord's Day given completely to worship," some congregations began to call for legislation to regulate Sunday activities. Without reservation, many Christians advocated the passage of "blue laws." Considerable effort was spent working for laws to prevent "the running of trains and the delivery of mail" on Sunday. While the sabbatarians constantly lost ground, the traditional Sunday was preserved in Tennessee, as well as in other southern states, to a greater extent than in the remainder of the nation.

The extensive attention given to local church activities reflected the crystallization of a self-conscious sectional society which most of Tennessee shared with the rest of the South. Further, the emphasis on the "spirituality of the church," reflecting the sub-culture that looked in upon itself, made anything that originated outside the region anathema. This focus on local affairs, combined with the distrust of outside influences, effectively insulated Tennessee against ideas and practices that began beyond the state. Consequently, significant religious movements, such as Protestant Liberalism and the Social Gospel, which were causing dramatic upheavals in American Protestantism, had hardly any impact upon most Tennessee congregations.

Protestant Liberalism, relying heavily on ideas imported from Germany, challenged the validity of the Bible as the final authority in matters of Christian faith and practice. Some of the scholars cast doubt on the accepted authorship of certain books of the Bible and also declared that several traditionally accepted biblical events were not supported by scientific findings. Making use of scientific investigation and historical analysis, these scholars made sure that no part of the Bible escaped their critical examination. The concepts, which later became known as form criticism, higher criticism, and lower criticism, were key ideas in the works of liberal scholars. A new climate had been created, and it had serious repercussions for Protestantism.

But Tennessee church members were sheltered from the circulation of these teachings, which cast doubt on the validity of the ultimate sources of Protestant truth. The views of those who declared the Bible untrustworthy did not penetrate the state. When a liberal voice dared to be heard, it was quickly silenced. The Methodist trustees of Vanderbilt University, for example, abruptly cut short Professor Alexander Winchell's visiting lectureship in zoology when the Darwinian element of his teaching became known. The impact of liberalism was left for a later day.

The Social Gospel, called by some America's major contribution to world Protestantism, was the other monumental movement from which Tennessee church members were sheltered. Primarily an effort to address the evils of urbanized industrialism and to present a Christian alternative to Socialism, the movement emerged when some northern church leaders attempted to solve contemporary problems using economic prescriptions and the tools of political scientists. Not concerned with issues of doctrine in the usual sense, the leaders focused on contemporary social and economic problems which pointed to what they considered the neglected social teachings of Jesus. The central article in their new faith was the Kingdom of God—defined as fulfilling the will of God in the earthly life of man. The mission of the church became that of Christianizing the social order. Sin was interpreted in terms of social maladjustments and salvation as social reform. Man became God's partner in the reconstruction of society.

Largely a northern movement, the Social Gospel made few inroads into Tennessee. The only activity that approached embodying any of its concepts was the Rugby settlement, established in 1880 on the Tennessee plateau by Thomas Hughes, an English Christian Socialist. Designed as a community to provide social improvement of young Englishmen who had been displaced by inheritance laws and economic depression, Rugby was a novel scheme. Its sponsors hoped to interest Tennessee Episcopalians in its support, but failed, due in part to the objections of Bishop Charles Quintard, former Confederate chaplain and the state's Episcopal leader, who would not deviate from his position of keeping the church aloof from civil concerns. Conservative Protestantism ruled in Tennessee, even among Episcopalians.

The failure of Tennessee churches to respond to the Social Gospel did not mean they were devoid of interest in social concerns. Although the

fear of a "politicized church" existed and the continued emphasis on revivalism tended to divert attention from secular affairs, many ministers,
along with some church members, began discussions of public issues
that had moral implications. Slowly, the emphasis on personal religion
was supplemented by subdued pronouncements on the moral dimen-
sions of public issues. As social awareness developed, there were some
attempts to influence social behavior. More social problems were no-
ticed, however, than were solved. The primary purpose of the church
remained the proclamation of the Gospel to the sinner; involvement in
discussions and action on social issues was relegated to a position of secondary importance.

A social issue of paramount importance was the relationship between
the races. While efforts had been made to convince people of the possibility of a satisfactory adjustment between the races, there was little inclination by whites to revise the conception of the subordinate place of
blacks in society. Blacks were expected to continue in an inferior and
subordinate relationship, and their desperate plight was not fully com-
prehended. Among even enlightened whites there was hardly more than
a determination to see that blacks had opportunity to hear the Gospel.
Paternalistic efforts continued to support educational enterprises, primarily those that trained black preachers and teachers to serve black
people. While the white churches supported the prevailing customs in
race relations, they did work for black rights. Against the Ku Klux Klan
— which more whites feared than supported — and lynchings, many congregations stood forth as outspoken champions of the personal safety of
blacks, demanding for them the impartial protection of the law and the
enjoyment of their citizenship. But basically the congregations did not
see, or want to see, the inherent contradiction between the defense of a
caste system based on color and the Christian principle of the brother-
hood of man, the worth of the individual, and the oneness of all peoples
in the sight of God.

The most encouraging endeavor in race relations was the effort of
some churches to extend their support to those of all races who were deprived of nominal family life. In establishing agencies to care for the
widows and orphans, an endeavor met at first by some local prejudice,
the churches manifested undeniable humanitarian aims. But these, and
related efforts, never reached a point where church people saw the need
for basic social reform.

The churches moved again into the social arena when they addressed
social evils that had personal moral or religious implications for the in-

dividual. Primarily concerned with the leisure-time activities of its members, the churches in taking a position on these issues exercised a leavening influence on society. The public evils most frequently excoriated were the same ones that had concerned the churches in earlier periods, but which were more prevalent now, more acceptable, and more freely conducive to immorality. Lying, stealing, and adultery were uniformly forbidden. The growing attractiveness of worldly amusements — dancing, theater going, card playing, novel reading — received both increased condemnation and efforts to banish them.

Among the amusements most often criticized, dancing was viewed as the cardinal sin next to drinking. Declared to be the "favored amusement of the profane" and the very "highest expression of the world's worldliness," no church member dared to dance publicly. The theater was no less feared and was referred to as the "synagogue of satan." One minister declared that "if the scriptures are to be obeyed the theater must be avoided." Theaters were condemned because of the vulgar language that surrounded them, and criticism of other kinds of commercial entertainment never ebbed. Because it motivated gambling, horse racing was also frequently denounced. Church members were urged to read in moderation wholesome novels and other acceptable secular materials. The writings of the "godless" Tolstoy, Zola, and Whitman were taboo, along with the popular *Police Gazette* and the "dime novel."

With the rise of organized and professional sports, churches came to look with growing disdain upon some of the popular athletic diversions of the time. Churches feared the effects of football, baseball, and boxing upon the rising generations. Because of the frequency with which people attended or participated in sporting events on Sunday, church people inevitably associated these sports with wrongdoing. When intercollegiate football and baseball games were criticized for promoting demoralizing and brutalizing tendencies, church-supported schools moved to prohibit them.

The most vigorous and dramatic efforts for enforced personal and social morality were those directed against the consumption of intoxicants. The campaign against the liquor traffic, the Tennessee equivalent of the Social Gospel, moved the church across a boundary that had been so studiously avoided — involvement in politics. The fight against excessive consumption of liquor was not new. There had been attacks early in the nineteenth century and a crusade was well underway by the second quarter of the century, with the organization of temperance societies, agencies that worked primarily to secure total abstinence from the use of intoxicating beverages. But the war had crippled temperance activity in Tennessee and aggravated intemperance. When hostilities ceased, drunkenness — partially stimulated by despondence over the future — appeared to be increasing rapidly, and social drinking became prevalent. As excessive drinking increased so did vulgar activity and acts of violence. Drunkenness and its attendant evils were reported to be common among all classes of society, church members as well as others.

Confronted by this state of affairs, many Tennessee church leaders, and a sizeable group of temperance-minded women, began to exert themselves vigorously to banish the use of whiskey. All were convinced that drunkenness was the cardinal sin in the state. In an unrelenting war, intemperance was fought as the "great crime of the century."

With the aim of halting completely the consumption of intoxicating beverages, the temperance fight was soon at full force. The Methodists took the leadership. In 1876 a major portion of the sessions of both the northern and southern Holston conferences was devoted to the cause of temperance. Declaring that the use of intoxicants in any way was immoral, Methodist ministers were urged to preach regularly on the evils of drink. Ministers in other denominations also took strong stands. And the churches provided large quotas to the membership of the Sons of Temperance, the Order of Good Templars, the Friends of Temperance, and the Woman's Christian Temperance Union. In Knoxville, the St. Mary's Catholic Total Abstinence Society was formed to train Catholic youth "in the path of morality and sobriety." Working together, these groups brought pressure to bear, and in 1877 the Four Mile Law was passed. The law — which prohibited the sale of liquor within four miles of any chartered school outside an incorporated town — was later amended to become the instrument for drying up the entire state.

The Four Mile Law was a milestone. With its passage, the temperance forces, led by the churches, gradually ceased to rely primarily on sermons, prayers, and moral persuasion and sought to achieve their objectives chiefly through legislation. Many thought this constituted political interference. It did. Churches were now actively involved in politics. Even the Baptists, strongest advocates of separation of church and state, were not hesitant in using the powers of government in the cause of temperance; the only issue was how to do it. Passage of local option measures was supported, but the main thrust was to secure prohibition by state constitutional amendment. The milder temperance movement, primarily advocating abstinence by persuasion, was replaced by an effort to influence legislation.

As an issue involving both morals and politics, the prohibition movement prompted many public statements by church leaders and denominational officials. In 1883 the Holston Conference of the Southern
Methodist denomination voted to work not just for state but for national prohibition as well. Two years later, the Tennessee conference urged
all of its members to support the movement. Methodists in the Lebanon
area declared that prohibition was the cause "of God and humanity."

Although believing that moral persuasion was an effective way to get
rid of whiskey, the Baptists, too, came to support legal action. Churches
and associations regularly petitioned for the enacting of laws abolishing
the saloon, the symbol of the enemy. Both the Presbyterian Church,
U.S.A. and the Cumberland Presbyterian called for constitutional prohibition. Only the Roman Catholics, Episcopalians, and the Presbyterian Church, U.S. refrained from an endorsement of legal action. Leaders in these bodies stated that legislation limiting personal freedom
would promote dishonesty, hypocrisy, and disrespect for the law. In the
Christian Church there was controversy. Although a great deal of agitation existed, most members sided with David Lipscomb, editor of the
Gospel Advocate, who felt that God in some way would destroy the evil
of whiskey without Christian participation in politics. His influence was
strong enough to keep the Christian Church from joining wholeheartedly in the campaign to abolish whiskey legally. Lipscomb, however,
was never as passive as some thought him to be; his position was consis-
tent with his deep conviction about separation of church and state.

The prohibition issue led some church members to question the long
established practice of serving wine at communion services. Controversy developed over whether to use wine or grape juice. Among the
Baptists, to resolve the dilemma, the "two wine" theory was advanced. It
held that both fermented and unfermented grape juices were in common
use in the time of Jesus, and that He drank only the unfermented variety.
To avoid discord, the Baptists agreed to disagree. At their Tennessee
State Convention in 1891, they promptly tabled the following resolution: "*Resolved,* that in the observance of the ordinance of the Lord's
Supper, the unfermented juice of some grapes should be used and not alcoholic wines." Others were more abrupt. When Bishop Quintard found
that a minister of an Episcopal church in the Tennessee diocese had sub-
stituted grape juice for the sacramental wine, the Bishop poured the grape
juice on the ground, demanded and received wine, rebuked the minister,
and then lectured the congregation on the use of wine in the communion
service. People in other denominations debated the issue; most who expressed an opinion favored using unfermented grape juice.

The movement reached a climax in the state during 1887, with an all-out drive to secure the adoption of a prohibition amendment. The Methodists, Baptists, Presbyterians, U.S.A., and Cumberland Presbyterians worked hard for the state constitutional amendment and urged fellow citizens to support their efforts. All the while, David Lipscomb urged Christian Church members to stay away from the polls, although he permitted discussion of the issue in the *Gospel Advocate.* During the campaign, many ministers came in for more than their share of coarse criticism. One periodical declared that the contest had "narrowed down to an issue between the saloon and the practical preachers—the two chief spirited nuisances of the age." When the issue was put to a vote, and the majority expressed an opposition to prohibition, some felt that the active participation of clergymen had injured rather than helped the cause.

The political side of the movement probably reached one of its highest points in 1890, when the Prohibition party, organized in Tennessee in 1883, nominated David Kelley, the colorful Methodist minister at Gallatin, to run for governor. Kelley entered the campaign with enthusiasm and denounced unsparingly the position of the two major parties on the issue. The Methodist conferences were expected to endorse Kelley. But not only did they refuse to do so, the Tennessee conference even took disciplinary action against Kelley for leaving his church to campaign without prior approval of the conference. He was suspended from the ministry for six months, an action which aroused a storm of protest. The General Conference of the Methodist Church, however, reversed the ill-advised action. Racism was injected into the campaign when Kelley was denounced by the *Nashville American* as a "Negro lover." Ironically, earlier, in an effort to turn blacks against prohibition, the *Memphis Watchman,* a black newspaper, had declared: "Prohibition is a slave law, as it puts some in bondage and leaves others to do as they please." This fear prompted another black to say: "I fought the rebels for my freedom, and I'll fight again before I will let the prohibitionists take away my rights." Although he did not win the governorship, or even come close, Kelley received the largest vote ever polled by the Prohibition party in Tennessee.

Church people continued their crusade. The Methodists remained the most outspoken. The Tennessee Baptist Convention declared: "*The Saloon Must Go.*" The Tennessee Christian Missionary Society, organized in 1889 by a liberal faction of the Christian Church, took a decided stand for prohibition. The other denominations did not deviate from their previous position. When legislation they supported was voted down in 1891, 1893, and 1895, they were stimulated to make greater efforts.

The churches remained in the vanguard of the prohibition movement, but the crusade, for all of the energies expended, was proving to be a discouraging endeavor. While well organized, the prohibition forces had hardly been a match for the better organized "liquor men" who seemed to be in league with the courts, established political parties, and law enforcement agencies. In the closing year of the century, the Anti-Saloon League was organized; working through it, the Baptists, Methodists, Presbyterians, U.S.A., and Cumberland Presbyterians mounted a last ditch effort and secured some favorable legislation. This spawned another decade of intense agitation—and success. Statewide prohibition became law in 1909. Church people rejoiced, seeing it as the fulfillment of many dreams and much hard work. Many thought it would remove forever the curse of intoxicating beverages and the tragedies spawned by their use. But experience proved them wrong.

Apart from achieving the legal ban on whiskey, the prohibition movement exposed the existence of a division within the Christian Church. As is often the case, the division issues were more cultural than theological. The suspicions and distrust that led to separation initially appeared during the Civil War when the American Christian Missionary Society, the chief agency of the loosely structured denomination, passed highly politically motivated resolutions, during sessions in Cincinnati, endorsing the Union and supporting the armies that were defending the country against "armed traitors." At war's end another offensive resolution, critical of the South, was voted; for some Tennessee members of the Christian Church it kept ablaze the strong sectional sentiment aroused by the earlier resolutions and deepened the opposition to missionary societies. Because of the resolution, leaders like David Lipscomb now became militant opponents of missionary organizations.

The animosity toward societies was combined with opposition to the tendencies of some congregations, particularly urban ones, to adjust to cultural influences. Accommodation was manifested in a congregation housing itself in a costly and elegant edifice, using an expensive musical instrument during worship, and being led by a trained, salaried, resident minister.

As the decade of the 1880s unfolded, it was quite apparent that rigid positions were being taken on the issues of missionary societies and cultural accommodations. On one side were rural conservative members, led primarily by David Lipscomb through the *Gospel Advocate,* who opposed societies and accommodation. On the other side were East Tennessee churches that, because of their long-standing Unionist sentiments that allied them with the northern viewpoint, supported missionary societies, and the urban congregations across the state, which were practitioners of accommodation. These two groups gradually fused in opposition to the conservative, rural group. Statements and reports from either the Lipscomb-led faction or the East Tennessee-urban coalition served to widen the existing chasm.

The crucial issue proved to be the missionary society, climaxing in 1889, when the East Tennessee congregations, along with the urban ones, organized the Tennessee Christian Missionary Society. The political dimension of the society also was demonstrated when it immediately adopted a statement in support of the prohibition movement. From then on, those who supported the programs it represented and those who opposed them avoided contact. For all purposes, division had been accomplished. When the Religious Census of 1906 recorded 42,297 members of the Churches of Christ, mainly rural and in Middle and West Tennessee, and 14,960 Christian Church members, it was making a matter of record a separation that had existed for almost two decades.

As the Christian Church experienced division, the Cumberland Presbyterians attempted merger. The Cumberland Presbyterians, with their greatest strength in Tennessee, initiated reunion conversations with the Presbyterian Church, U.S.A. (popularly known as the Northern Presbyterian Church), entrenched in East Tennessee, in the opening years of the twentieth century. Groups in each of the denominations had been discussing consolidation for years. They appeared to be natural partners. While the Cumberland Presbyterians and the Presbyterian Church, U.S. (Southern Presbyterian Church) appeared to be in almost constant disagreement, the Cumberland and Northern Presbyterians had been taking similar positions on issues, including theology. So it came as no surprise when a plan was advanced in 1904. The name of the reunited church was to be the Presbyterian Church in the United States of America. The coalition was to be on the basis of the Confession of Faith of the Presbyterian Church in the United States of America, as revised in 1903. But to some Cumberland Presbyterians, the plan appeared to be inequitable. Many Tennessee Cumberland Presbyterians were upset at the concessions they would be called upon to make. Both advocates and opponents organized their forces. The strongest opposition developed among the Cumberland Presbyterians in Middle and West Tennessee. When the issue came to a vote, only two of thirteen presbyteries in the state voted in the affirmative, but the numerical count of the total vote was closely in favor of consolidation. The northern Presbyterians, meanwhile, voted convincingly for merger, including the presbyteries in Tennessee. In 1906, union was declared to be in effect, the Cumberland Presbyterian Church was now combined with the Presbyterian Church in the United States of America as one church. But all was not well.

Many who had opposed the action could not bring themselves to become a part of the united denomination. Instead, they were determined to continue as Cumberland Presbyterians. Their strongest support was in the middle and western areas of Tennessee. The Obion Presbytery became the first to declare itself a part of the continuing Cumberland Presbyterian Church. Other Tennessee presbyteries took similar positions. The Presbyterian Church, U.S.A. countered the Cumberland group at each stage. Lines were drawn at the presbyterial level and a contest developed for the allegiance of the people. The competition was complicated by a struggle over property rights which eventually reached the civil courts, with ultimate settlements generally favorable to the Cumberlands. The Cumberlands grew steadily, and in 1907 the General Assembly of the Cumberland Presbyterian Church met at the birthplace of the original denomination in Dickson County. There, the assembly was reminded, at the beginning of the nineteenth century the Cumberland Presbyterian Church had been born. Now, at the beginning of the twentieth century, it was being "born again."

Never had the churches been more involved in the total life of the state than in the last quarter of the nineteenth century. As accelerated attention was focused on evangelistic efforts to win new converts and on congregational activities to nurture them, there was an abundance of zeal for programs beyond the sanctuary. Churches that had normally unlocked their doors only on Sunday threw them open every day of the week for planning sessions that addressed some of the social issues that had moral or religious implications and the public issues that had moral overtones. While many felt the churches had no business concerning themselves with such problems, the projects to influence — and in some instances enforce — social behavior were tackled with exuberance. Some warned of the consequences of forsaking the old-fashioned religion, but a powerful "new style" had emerged. It was a "style" destined to characterize a great deal of church life well into the twentieth century.

Changes in Methodist architecture are seen in a montage of buildings of McKendree Methodist Church, named for William McKendree, who resided in Tennessee during his tenure as bishop.

1790

1812 – 1818

BISHOP M?KENDREE

818-1833

1833 – 1876

1879 1905

6. Between Two World Wars

Tennessee congregations cheered the entry of the United States into World War I. America's commitment to the conflict across the Atlantic came as no surprise. With trumpets blowing and the air filled with banners, Tennessee churches, along with the rest, since the Spanish American War — the "little war" that rationalized imperialism as a missionary obligation — had given support to one campaign after another to make the twentieth century the Christian century. As the country had moved from the little war to the great war, without breaking gait, moral idealism and an abundance of zeal had found expression in the Laymen's Missionary Campaign, World Student Christian Federation, Student Volunteer Movement, Men and Religion Forward Movement, and the Movement for World Peace. When the declaration was made to fight in Europe, all of the enthusiasm and exuberance generated by these peaceful crusaders was diverted into the one great crusade to end war and make the world safe for democracy and Christianity. As the church militant marched out and into a "holy war" with unprecedented fervor, hardly a member or minister raised a voice in opposition.

As the processes of government moved to create a fighting force from the raw material of men, preachers presented arms. Swept up in the excitement of the hour, far more of the state's ministers volunteered to accompany the troops as chaplains and YMCA workers than could be used. Clerics who did not work among the military did not have to worry about what to preach: sermon outlines were sent to them by government propaganda agencies, along with illustrations from which selections could be made, including atrocity stories. Meanwhile, the separation of church and state was suspended as the cross and flag were united in common service. Churches were utilized for all sorts of meetings, most of them having some bearing on the war. Special meetings for the dedication of service flags were extremely popular. Many congregations virtually became recruiting centers and propaganda agencies. Amid the display of service flags, Liberty Bonds and War Saving Stamps were hawked in crowded sanctuaries. There were numerous patriotic gatherings. No one could deny that the church was in the forefront as the enemy was fought with both ideas and weapons.

In November 1918 the big guns were silenced. War was over. There were services of rejoicing across the state. They had hardly concluded, however, when the idealism with which the nation had entered the war was abruptly shattered. Reports surfaced of secret agreements and desire for revenge that buried many hopes. The vindictiveness of the French and the reluctance of the British stymied efforts by the President of the United States to bring about a just and honorable peace. The rude awakening of Americans was followed by a sense of betrayal. Since the war had been supported at such a high emotional level, disillusionment set in when Americans discovered their ideals and good intentions scoffed at as unrealistic. Isolationism was the reaction. It was perfectly normal. When Warren Harding, in the presidential campaign of 1920, promised a return to what he called "normalcy," most citizens were ready to march to the beat of those drums. Harding's summons to put aside idealistic concerns mirrored the mood of a tired, disillusioned, and disenchanted people.

Declining idealism, accompanied by a resurgence of nationalism, led to a concentration once again on local church activities. More and more stress was placed on the growth and development of the local congregation. In the urban areas, especially Memphis and Nashville, new techniques were used to persuade people to come to church. Strategically placed billboards, lighted sign boards, weekly parish papers, and printed Sunday bulletins urged citizens to join the church for the sake of the community. As more members were brought in and the churches grew, many sanctuaries were remodeled, others were enlarged, and a large number of new edifices, for the most part gothic in design, were constructed. Prosperity carried over into increased support for denominational colleges, benevolent programs, and health care institutions. But there was hardly any support for religious enterprises beyond the state. Campaigns by the Presbyterians, Methodists, Baptists, and Christian churches, for example, to raise funds for worldwide Christian advances were all dismal failures.

Many local churches discovered they were not the only organization asking for the support of the people in improving the moral and ethical level of the community. Rotary, Kiwanis, and Lions clubs sprang up, almost overnight, all across the state. These and other civic clubs became additional organizations competing for the primary loyalties of men in the sponsorship of many worthy enterprises. Once a week these club members dined together, became involved in much hilarity, and heard speeches on every conceivable subject. Occasionally, a church member, who also held club membership, would withdraw from active church participation in favor of club activity. One Nashvillian justified such a move by declaring that what he heard in Sunday sermons was the same thing he heard in weekly Rotary speeches, and since he could enjoy a meal and a cigar at the Rotary meeting, he chose it over the worship services. But fortunately, most all civic club members were also staunch supporters of the church.

Another organization reflecting the reaction born of postwar disillusionment — and impinging on church life but belonging to an entirely different category from the civic clubs — was the Ku Klux Klan. Using the name of the organization that first emerged in Tennessee at the end of the Civil War, the new Klan, founded in 1915, amounted to nothing until the end of World War I, when it became the very hallmark of reaction. Appealing to patriotism, this agency of organized bigotry carried on a program of terror and torture against blacks and occasionally against Roman Catholics and Jews. In addition to these minority groups, village reprobates and "fallen" women also felt the sting of the Klan's displeasure. Membership in the Klan was open only to white Protestant men. Baptists, together with members of the Methodist and Christian churches, were accused of giving the Klan its strongest support in Tennessee. Some church people did join; so did a few clergymen. Others gave it tacit support. Most of the clergy, however, in obscure parishes as well as in city cathedrals, had both the courage and common sense to lead their congregations in condemnation of the organization. Not a single denominational periodical in the state endorsed the Klan; most vigorously denounced it. The Nashville *Christian Advocate* declared the methods of the Klan to be dangerous and urged Methodists not to be "duped by any organization that appealed to passion and prejudice." The *Presbyterian Advance* labeled the Klan the "essence of mobocracy" and called it un-American, un-Christian, and unnecessary. The editor felt that the churches were "having troubles enough of their own without meddling in those of the Klan," an organization that violated "every basic precept of the religion of Jesus." The Klan remained active, however, and the churches had to deal with its presence for years to come, principally by denouncing its bigoted activities.

In the period of postwar reaction, the center of the stage was occupied, however, by the "fundamentalist-modernist controversy," a debate that was late in getting to Tennessee. Modernism, directly linked with European scholarship, and questioning the reliability and authority of Scripture, had proponents among scholars and preachers outside the state from the latter part of the nineteenth century onward. The counteroffensive by the fundamentalists — setting forth the "fundamental" doctrines of the verbal inerrancy of Scripture, the virgin birth of Jesus, the physical resurrection, the physical second coming of Christ, and substitutionary atonement — was also carried on by groups and individuals beyond Tennessee. Early in the twentieth century, the battlelines had been mapped. After a wartime moratorium, the old issues were rekindled. More convinced than ever that the Bible was being destroyed by modernism, the fundamentalists seized the initiative. Capitalizing on the postwar reaction to anything European, including theological liberalism, the fundamentalists, in 1919, organized the World's Christian Fundamentals Association and declared war on "counterfeit Christianity." The resulting controversy became a struggle for ecclesiastical control, and the intensity varied in direct proportion to the strength of theological liberalism in a particular denomination.

In Tennessee, modernism did not constitute a threat in any denomination, and the controversy remained relatively peaceful compared to other regions. Activity centered on advancing fundamentalism within the denominations, especially the Baptist and Presbyterian. Beyond the denominations, the program of the fundamentalists took a distinct form: a determined effort to prevent public schools and colleges from teaching scientific theories which contradicted scripture, specifically Darwin's theory of evolution. Since Darwinism was deemed incompatible with the traditional interpretation of the Bible, fundamentalists assumed the task of "driving it from the state."

The campaign to awaken the rank and file Christians and get the teaching of Darwinism outlawed accelerated when William Riley, president of the World's Christian Fundamentals Association, toured Tennessee in 1923. The following year, William Jennings Bryan, the Great Commoner and unsuccessful presidential candidate on several occasions, delivered a lecture in Nashville on the subject "Is the Bible True?" Bryan reassured his listeners that the Bible was, indeed, true and without error from cover to cover. The lecture was printed and when the 1925 session of the General Assembly convened, copies of the speech were given to legislators in the hope of gaining support for anti-evolution legislation.

Such efforts were rewarded when on January 20, 1925, Senator John A. Shelton of Savannah introduced a bill to "prohibit the teaching of evolution in public schools." The next day a similar measure was introduced in the House of Representatives by John Butler, a member of the Primitive Baptist church from Macon County. Butler's proposal was designed to prohibit any public school teacher from teaching "any theory that denies the story of the Divine Creation of man as taught in the Bible, and to teach instead that man descended from a lower order of animals."

Most church people applauded the proposed legislation. But there were exceptions. Richard Qwensby, for example, minister of the First Methodist Church in Columbia, declared in a sermon that the legislators were "making monkeys of themselves," and that he did not "believe a state legislature could possibly devise a more asinine performance." The House took official cognizance of this slur on its integrity and gave its retort in a resolution which declared the pastor's remarks to be "unfair, unchristianlike and unpatriotic." The resolution further asserted that "if Protestant ministers in the state . . . would confine themselves . . . to preaching . . . the gospel . . . as found in the Bible . . . there would be no need for public demand for legislation on the teaching of evolution."

By March the bill introduced by Senator Shelton had been tabled in favor of the Butler bill. As the bill was being debated, a petition from some Nashville religious leaders, urging rejection, was read to the Senate. These clerics were immediately criticized. The pastor of the Eastland Baptist Church in a letter to the *Tennessean* declared that "fathers and mothers resent the action of the preachers who signed the letter asking the state senate not to pass the anti-evolution bill." The elders of the Hohenwald Church of Christ requested the same paper to publish their official endorsement of the action of the legislature. The Baptist Pastors Council of Nashville, in behalf of "ten thousand laymen of twenty local churches" supported the anti-evolution legislation.

When the final vote was taken, the bill was easily approved by a General Assembly made up primarily of Methodists, followed by Baptists and Presbyterians, respectively. In signing the Butler bill, Governor Austin Peay, himself a Baptist, termed the law a "protest against an irreligious tendency to exalt so called science, and deny the Bible in some schools and quarters." The governor added: "Right or wrong, there is a deep and widespread belief that something is shaking the fundamentals of the country, both in religion and morals. It is the opinion of many that an abandonment of the old fashioned faith and belief in the Bible is our trouble to a large degree. It is my own belief."

While the new law was widely cheered, it was also deeply resented, especially by college students. At the University of Tennessee a petition addressed to "our dear legislators" was circulated on the campus. In it the students sarcastically thanked their representatives for their "faithful service to the public" in passing the law. Further, the petition suggested that the law of gravity be amended, and asked that something "be done about the excessive speed of light." W.R. Cole, Jr., a Vanderbilt student, in a letter to the *New York Times,* declared that "The alumni, students and faculty of Vanderbilt are all ashamed of the well meaning ignorance and narrowness that has put Tennessee in such a ridiculous position in the eyes of the world."

The statute was soon tested. John Scopes, a teacher at Rhea County High School, Dayton, in a classroom presentation made reference to Darwinism, was reported and then indicted for violating the new Tennessee antievolution law. In the course of a few days in July 1925 over two million words were telegraphed out of Dayton reporting on the trial of Scopes, primarily because of the confrontation between William Jennings Bryan, present to assist the state in the presentation, and Clarence Darrow, attorney for the defense. The trial itself bore more resemblance to a camp meeting than a legal process. The presiding judge opened the trial by offering prayer in a session that met on the courthouse lawn because of the heat. Darrow objected on the ground that it was likely to prejudice the case against the defendant. At issue in the trial was the legality of teaching evolution; in the minds of the many observers, however, at stake was the defense of the "fundamental" doctrines of Christianity, especially the inerrant inspiration of the Bible. Bryan, in prosecuting the case, said evolution was the eternal enemy of Christianity; it made God unnecessary; it denied the Bible; and it destroyed all belief in the supernatural. Darrow, for his part, attempted to make Bryan appear ridiculous and submitted him to a mocking examination.

Scopes was found guilty and an appeal to the State Supreme Court upheld the constitutionality of the law. A week after the trial, and still in Dayton, Bryan died, a victim of the heat and stress. In his memory, admirers contributed funds to establish at Dayton, William Jennings Bryan University, an institution dedicated to preserve and defend the "fundamentals" of the Christian religion.

The events surrounding the trial of John Scopes were still being widely discussed when the religious forces were caught up in more excitement — the presidential campaign of 1928. Months before the nominating convention of the two parties, speculation began to center on Alfred Smith, a Roman Catholic from New York, as the likely nominee for the Demo-

crats. For Tennessee church members, Democrats and Republicans alike, the prospect of Smith's becoming President was ominously disturbing, especially in light of his known advocacy of repeal of the Eighteenth Amendment. Having spoken often, in well-publicized addresses, of the need for fundamental changes in the provision for national prohibition, Smith was perceived as a threat. The drive for prohibition in the state had enlisted the interest and enthusiasm of the churches more than any other movement, and church people were convinced that any effort to alter it would throw the state back into the clutches of the "grossly materialistic liquor traffic" and the evils associated with it. Smith's nomination was virtually assured by September 1927, when a caucus of Democrats, representing eight Pacific and mountain states, endorsed his candidacy. With that, religious leaders who were Democrats worked diligently to make sure a dry platform was voted by the nominating convention. But Smith, in accepting the nomination, stated he would work for, if elected, changes in the provisions of the Eighteenth Amendment. This made certain, as the *Nashville Tennessean* correctly predicted, that the "liquor question was to be a monstrous moral issue" in the campaign.

The convention had hardly adjourned until the aroused religious forces in the state began the campaign to deny Smith the presidency. Seeking office in a period of booming prosperity, with a Republican occupant in the White House, Smith was faced with a difficult prospect; while prosperity was a major item, prohibition was the issue of transcendent importance for Tennesseans. The threat to prohibition was a matter of gravest concern, especially to Baptists and Methodists. Comprising almost three-quarters of the state's church membership, they constituted a potent force, and in the interest of the moral welfare of the state, they felt justified in abandoning the traditional doctrine of separation of church and state to lead the fight against Smith.

Methodist Bishop Horace DuBose of Nashville, who had unsuccessfully attempted to block the nomination, led the Methodists in opposing Smith, declaring it was "no longer a political campaign, but a moral revolution." The bishop was abiding by a statement he had issued earlier, affirming his intention of waging a militant fight against Smith on the grounds of his prohibition policy. During the campaign, however, it was more a matter of representing the constituency than leading it. The mem-

Scene at Dayton courtroom during Scopes trial as William Jennings Bryan delivered his speech defending the Bible.

bership of the three Methodist conferences, almost a third of the state's total church membership, already held a strong anti-Smith position; when they listened to the bishop's warning they nodded their heads in approval. What they heard was in accord with their own convictions.

The bishop was aided by the two Methodist periodicals published in the state, the *Christian Advocate* at Nashville and the *Methodist Advocate* at Jackson. While both strongly supported prohibition and opposed Smith, the *Christian Advocate* was more moderate in its statements and editorial policy. The editor of the *Methodist Advocate*, extreme in his opposition, on two occasions invoked higher authorities to urge a vote against Smith. In one issue he asked, "How would Jesus vote?" And in another, "Where would Bryan stand?" In both cases the conclusion was against Smith. The editor was constantly being congratulated for his fight "against 'Alcohol Smith.'"

Methodist clergymen needed little encouragement to become active in the campaign. Because it involved electing a President who did not share their views on prohibition, they felt it a moral issue on which they were obligated to speak. Clergymen increased the number of sermons devoted to the preservation of prohibition, and in opposition to Smith. From rural circuits to urban pulpits, prohibition was made the paramount issue in the race for the presidency.

In the zeal to maintain prohibition the Baptists took second place to no other religious group; and the threat to prohibition accounted for the almost unanimous opposition of Baptists to Smith's candidacy. Opposition was dramatized in the resolutions of associations, in editorials, and in the sermons of pastors. The majority of the 63 Baptist associations in the state passed resolutions declaring their campaign against Smith to be primarily moral rather than political — "a contest between the prohibition forces and the liquor traffic." The editor of the *Baptist and Reflector,* the state's Southern Baptist journal, reported he could not "accept Mr. Smith on several counts," but the primary battle was "against his prohibition . . . policies." He represented the views of his readers. Another editor was more emphatic: "I regard the Eighteenth Amendment as the greatest piece of moral legislation in the history of government, and I cannot and will not stand idly by and see Governor Smith . . . destroy this." Ministers with pulpits were the most audible spokesmen for the Smith opposition, and scarcely a Baptist congregation could avoid hearing sermons related in some way to the role of prohibition in the political campaign. Additionally, Baptists gave unreserved backing to the activities of the Anti-Saloon League and the WCTU. Baptist money passed into the treasury of these organizations. So did that of Methodists. In support of these two programs, the state's leading religious bodies acted in rare concert.

No other Protestant denomination came close to matching the Methodist and Baptist in opposition to Smith. The Episcopal and Presbyterian bodies, ignoring the campaign as far as the state structure and religious periodicals were concerned, left their ministers and members free to act according to their own judgment. The Christian Church and Churches of Christ were too loosely structured to do anything officially. When an individual supported Smith, or opposed him, there was denominational freedom to speak out. Sometimes when ministers expressed their position it created scenes such as the one that took place in Camden a month before the election. The Reverend John Clark, a Presbyterian, mounted a box on the town's main street and began speaking against Smith. The Reverend Charles Taylor, a Christian Church minister who supported Smith, challenged some of Clark's statements. The ensuing debate was so heated that it took a sheriff and six deputies to prevent a riot.

The mobilization of opposition to Smith by the Methodists and Baptists, on an unprecedented scale primarily because of his stand on prohibition, made Democratic leaders and editors of secular newspapers supporting his candidacy aware that they faced difficulty in holding the line for the nominee. To convert a liability into an asset, there were deliberate attempts to make religion an issue: the assertion was that prohibition was being used as a cover for bigotry. One Democratic leader declared that Smith's stand on prohibition hurt him some, "but more frequently than not his 'wetness' was used as a cloak to screen the real objection to him, namely, his Catholicism." As late as November a Smith supporter in a Nashville speech said, "Prohibition is injected into this campaign to dignify bigotry." Not many were convinced by the rhetoric; one Baptist minister came closer to hitting the target when he said, "This business of dragging religion into the campaign is the old political game of covering up objectionable things by switching attention to false issues."

Smith's Catholicism was a sensitive issue — not as important as prohibition — and made him unacceptable to many Tennessee Protestants. The degree of anti-Catholicism varied, but the evidence is clear that being a Roman Catholic was a major liability. Most of those for whom Smith's religion was an issue presented their views openly, frankly, and did not resort to cowardly whispering campaigns. The arguments appeared to be on a higher level than bigotry. Catholicism was more an issue with Baptists than Methodists and more decisive for rural residents than urban dwellers. But it did not equal prohibition as a factor in the campaign. Bishop DuBose of the Methodist church spoke for most when he said, "I only oppose Governor Smith because he is against the 18th Amendment."

During these hectic weeks, the Roman Catholics, some 25,000 strong and ministered to by 55 priests, attempted to keep a low profile. But it was difficult. Smith's stand in favor of modifying prohibition aroused Protestant suspicion that the Roman Catholics were the sponsors of alternatives to prohibition. Old fears and prejudices, which had lain dormant, were awakened. Expressions of prejudice exerted considerable pressure upon the patience and tolerance of the state's Catholics. They had learned to live with a certain amount of intolerance, but the months of 1928 were unlike anything ever experienced before. Bishop Alphonse Smith, the leader of the Catholic church in Tennessee, attempted to keep the issues surrounding the campaign as quiet as possible. He exercised extreme caution to realize his aim, and the priests acted with dignity and restraint in guiding Catholics in the state through these troubled times.

When the votes were counted in the election, the balloting in heavily Democratic Tennessee—reflecting more a vote against Smith than in favor of Herbert Hoover—gave the Republican nominee a decisive majority. Many interpreted the outcome as a vindication of righteousness. But there was an uneasiness in victory. Many shared the sentiment of Bishop DuBose, who said, "I hope the church will never again be compelled to take the offensive in a political campaign." The bishop's words must have been remembered. While the Protestant forces with one massive effort had worked to prevent any abridgement of the prohibition laws in the election of 1928, they were incapable of preventing the voters in the election of 1932 from giving the state's electoral votes to the Democratic nominee, Franklin Roosevelt, a Protestant who advocated outright repeal of prohibition. In 1932, with an unpleasant choice between repeal of the Eighteenth Amendment (Democrats) and modification (Republicans), church people faced a dilemma and their activity was quite inhibited when compared to four years earlier. It was as if all their ammunition had been expended. Nor were they able to prevent the abandonment of statewide prohibition which subsequently followed the adoption of the Twenty-first Amendment, repealing the Eighteenth. In the election of 1928, the church forces had reached the high water mark on the liquor issue.

Between the two presidential elections, economic collapse came to Tennessee. With the rest of the nation, the state experienced the Great

Depression. The summer of 1929 witnessed the zenith of national prosperity, but in October a drastic downward movement occurred in the stock market. The plunge triggered a decline in all of American economic life. Industry and agriculture were both hit hard; plants closed and farm products piled up—hardly anyone had money with which to make purchases. In the months and years that followed, mortgages went unpaid; banks failed; transportation systems ground to a halt; unemployment increased staggeringly. While President Hoover declared that prosperity was just around the corner, things got steadily worse as the economic collapse the state shared with the rest of the nation worked its wrath on all classes and conditions of people and had wide-ranging religious ramifications. In 1932, after the public had fully grasped the seriousness of the situation, Franklin Roosevelt was elected overwhelmingly to the presidency in the hope he could do something. Upon assuming office, he inaugurated a large number of programs aimed at developing national recovery. Slowly the country did begin to recover, but as late as World War II, economic depression had not completely run its course.

Like a pall over the state, the Great Depression had a devastating effect on religious life. The financial impact was immediate. With widespread unemployment and prices of farm produce at rock bottom, there was a ravaging plunge in contributions both to the work of the local church and to denominational causes. Extremely careful use was made of the little money available; priority was given to preserving the ownership of church buildings.

In the prosperity following World War I, congregations had built new edifices, some quite large and expensive. Most were in the urban areas, but new, plain, simple buildings dotted the rural area as well. Chattanooga led in the building spree; during the early 1920s the Methodists alone erected ten new sanctuaries in Hamilton County. One of these, Centenary Methodist, was built at a cost of over $300,000. Knoxville almost equaled Chattanooga in new church structures and surpassed it in costly construction, with Centenary Methodist there taking over $425,000 to complete. With moneylenders anxious to make church loans, borrowed funds had been used in construction; when the depression came, many congregations found themselves with high debts. Centenary Methodist in Knoxville, for example, had an indebtedness of over $215,000 in 1930, out of an aggregate debt of $798,188 for all of the Methodist churches of Knoxville. The debts were heavy burdens, and it became the all-preoccupying purpose of many congregations simply to meet the debt obligations to avoid foreclosure. Most did, but over-zealous ministers and over-eager moneylenders had led some congregations to build far beyond their ability to pay; consequently, there were defaults. A few congregations, however, eventually were able to reclaim property on which they had defaulted.

After attending to the ownership of church property, efforts were made to provide a salary for the minister. With church contributions down by more than half, this was extremely difficult. Salaries were cut, some to the point of deprivation. Among the Methodists, the average ministerial salary had risen to the unprecedented figure of $2,300 by 1929. Shortly after the crash, the goal of $125 monthly for a minister with family proved unattainable. The situation was the same for ministers of the other denominations, except for the Baptists. As a group, Baptist pastors fared best. Outside of the urban areas, most of them supported their families by working at nonreligious jobs and served only additionally as pastor of a congregation. Desperation set in, however, when the wage-earning position was lost. Some churches had to sell minister's residences to meet debt payments, forcing the clergyman and his family to find living accommodations in rooms in the church normally used for offices and Sunday school classes. These were the fortunate ones; many had no church-supplied facilities at all. While some clergymen took drastic cuts in compensation, others were cut off entirely from church support. Some of the young ministers the churches had to let go found positions as chaplains in the Civilian Conservation Corps, one of the agencies devised by President Roosevelt to provide jobs for young men. Congregations of every denomination were forced to continue church activities without ministers, and in some instances churches, without pastors, closed. The desperate situation with reference to ministerial compensation dissuaded some youth who had intended to become ministers. Candidates for the ministry dropped to an all-time low. In the Tennessee Conference of the Methodist Church, for instance, only one person presented himself for candidacy in 1932; for each of the next two years, there was no one.

With congregations carrying building debts and endeavoring to support a minister, contributions to denominational missions and benevolent programs dropped sharply. Invariably these were the first funds cut by congregations when income declined. The drastic drop in mission and benevolent contributions by Southern Baptists in Tennessee was typical. In 1927 these denominational programs had been supported by contributions of over $336,000; but in 1933 the amount had plummeted to $163,000. Compounding the decreased financial support of denominational programs by churches was the total loss of reserve funds some agencies had deposited with banks that failed. One agency executive was but a voice in the chorus when he said, "Funds at our command are tragically depleted." Scarcity of money led to the consolidation of boards and agencies, curtailment or elimination of programs, tighter administration, reduced salaries, and the abolition of positions.

Denominational colleges and publishing houses also felt the full weight of the depression. As college enrollments were cut severely by the inability of students to meet expenses, income from endowments was curtailed, the substance of endowments eroded through bank failures, and, as direct church support ceased, the institutions were forced to make deep retrenchments in expenses and staff. The only additions to staffs were persons employed to raise funds; and they found it "simply impossible to secure pledges when most people were finding it difficult to keep the wolf away from the door." Some institutions did not survive. Among the more publicized closings were those of Centenary College, a Methodist school at Cleveland, and Burritt College, at Spencer, the only Christian Church college in the state.

Cancellation of subscriptions to periodicals and the drop in sales of religious literature placed the publishing enterprises in jeopardy. Borrowed funds kept most going but saddled them with debts that took years to remove. In spite of good management, most of the publishing operations came distressingly close to disaster.

As the depression wreaked havoc on the physical aspects of religious activities, church leaders began to predict that the deep physical, mental, and spiritual wounds that had been inflicted would bring the state to its knees in prayer and lead to a religious revival. This should have been a safe prediction, for previous economic reversals had spawned revivals. But the old adage of man's extremity being God's opportunity did not hold. The depression appeared to have destroyed self-confidence and given birth to despair. Unlike earlier periods where a scrutiny of religious needs motivated many to seek relief in religion, there was no surge of repentant people to the churches. Rather than a revival, there was a falling away, with 2,000 fewer congregations near the end of the depression than when it began. From shortly before the "crash" and until 1936, total church membership declined approximately 10 percent, from 1,018,033 to 918,809. Losses ran the gamut from 4 percent for the Christian Church to 31 percent for the Churches of Christ. (The statistics for the zealously autonomous Churches of Christ probably reflect the failure of local congregations to submit reports.) The two largest bodies, the Baptist and Methodist, had losses of about 16 percent each. The Presbyterian Church, U.S., with an increase of 11 percent, was the only major denomination in the state to report a gain. Although the churches made few or no gains in membership, more than likely the members who remained faithful grew in their depth of understanding of the meaning of suffering and sacrifice in the Christian life.

While the major denominations experienced a dramatic decline in congregational giving and in membership, something like a revival did take place within one segment of Protestantism—that made up of the Holiness and Pentecostal bodies. Highly moral and puritanical in their relationships, these bodies, quite "otherworldly" in their outlook, tend to benefit in periods of bleakness. Largely produced by hard times, the growing membership, seeing little chance for better conditions in this life, looked to the future where injustices and poverty would be overcome. During the depression these bodies enlarged their constituencies from among the disinherited, especially in the southeastern part of the state. The Church of the Nazarene more than doubled its membership during the depression. One branch of the Assemblies of God increased threefold. One Church of God body tripled its membership, and another, with headquarters in Cleveland, did the same. Rapidity of growth marked this segment of organized religion.

The depression played a role in one highly publicized religious event: The reunion of the northern and southern branches of the Methodist Church. Consultations looking toward unification had been going on for years, and involved several Methodist denominations. But the concept gained momentum in light of the economy that could be realized from the consolidation of duplicating boards, agencies, and staffs, and southern and northern Methodists ended their old alienation as reunion was endorsed enthusiastically by the state's Methodists in 1939 at a meeting in Nashville.

As the Methodists were planning to embrace peacefully, the Presbyterians were being torn by dissension. This time it was in Memphis and the issue was but another episode in the modernist-fundamentalist controversy. The disturbance centered around Charles Diehl, a scholarly man who had been pastor of the First Presbyterian Church in Clarksville before becoming president of Southwestern College, which he promptly moved from Clarksville to Memphis. On the Memphis campus, Dr. Diehl made the study of the Bible the capstone of the educational system and attempted to have it taught in the same scholarly fashion as were courses in Shakespeare, mathematics, and the sciences. In the fundamentalist atmosphere of West Tennessee, this prompted ten ministers from the Presbytery of Memphis to charge that President Diehl was "not what may be called sound in the faith" and that he did not believe in the full inspiration of the Scriptures. The board of directors of Southwestern and the Nashville Presbytery, of which he was a member, carefully investigated the charges and completely exonerated him. While the board and presbytery were satisfied with the solution to the charges, conservative Presbyterians were not. Church support dried up, and this, along with economic difficulties caused by the depression, made it appear the school might not survive. Generous friends, however, came to the aid of the institution, assuring its future.

One of the positive aspects of the depression was the opportunity it offered for improvement in black and white relations. Mutual distress drew people together, and neighbor discovered neighbor. With virtually everyone in trouble, a new awareness of community emerged. Religious periodicals called for greater cooperation between the races; the *Christian Advocate* urged a better "understanding and more sympathetic appreciation of the burden each has to bear." Near the end of the decade, the Federal Writers' Project, a Works Projects Administration agency to provide work for unemployed writers, reported that congregations were showing a "growing interest in promoting better understanding" between blacks and whites. But while there had been signs of improvement, a peaceful and equitable relationship was not achieved. Black clergy saw little hope for change in the system, and insisted that the only possibility for black advancement lay in cooperation between church leaders of the two races. The dreams did not find fulfillment. Probably the most far-reaching contribution to improved race relations was made by the YMCA graduate school in Nashville. Under the supervision of the director, W.A. Weatherford, blacks and whites attended conferences together, and in the integrated staff, spent summers working and studying, dealing particularly with the problems of race relations, lynchings, poverty, and the plight of the tenant farmer. The Highlander Folk School near Monteagle also brought together a group of young industrial workers and farm people of both races for workshops each year to explore similar issues.

Although Tennessee received many of the benefits of Roosevelt's New Deal, particularly through the Tennessee Valley Authority, some segments were still in the throes of depression when news reached the state, shortly after worshipers returned home from Sunday morning services on December 7, 1941, that United States military forces at Pearl Harbor had been bombed by the Japanese in a surprise air attack. The Japanese bombing brought the depression decade to an end and hurled the nation into war. As the country rushed into war, some church leaders were still suffering pangs of conscience for their endorsement of World War I as a holy crusade. The pacifist movement had grown in the state; the Methodists had declared not "to endorse, support, or . . . participate in war" again. The decisiveness of the Japanese ended the indecisiveness of the United States, and after the fateful event at Pearl Harbor even the pacifists reluctantly admitted the necessity of the nation's entry into armed conflict. But this was to be no holy war, no religious crusade; if the nation was to know any semblance of peace and justice, it was necessary to fight and put down a dangerous threat. Tennessee churches took their stand beside the government.

Church activities during World War II were different from what they had been in World War I. Churches did not become recruiting centers or headquarters for selling war bonds, nor were the pulpits used to fan the hatred and emotion of the people against real and imagined enemies. Within the state much church activity was directed toward providing service to soldiers and sailors. Churches in communities near military installations established programs to provide military personnel with meals, rest, and recreational activities—games, reading material—and occasionally places to sleep. The staffs of these operations, commonly called canteens, did everything possible to supply the military guests with some of the comforts of home and to assist them with personal problems. Supported by local as well as denominational funds, service centers were established to accommodate soldiers at Camp Forrest near Tullahoma, Camp Campbell near Clarksville, Camp Tyson near Paris, and sailors at Millington near Memphis. Social and recreational facilities were also operated for persons working at the shell-loading plant at Milan, the munitions plant at Tyner in Hamilton County, and the new airfield at Smyrna, near Nashville.

The abnormalities of war were apparent in other religious activities. Travel restrictions curtailed the work of denominational boards and agencies; missionary programs came to a virtual halt. Religious periodicals were filled with human interest stories from camps and battle areas. The restriction on building materials prevented construction of church structures. But wartime prosperity resulted in increased church offerings, and this provided a good opportunity to pay off debts accrued before and during the depression. Always there was the dramatic reminder of war: most sanctuaries had a service flag with a blue star for each member in service and a gold one for each who had died.

Probably the most notable way religious bodies supported persons in military service was through ministers who became chaplains and accompanied them on the land, on the sea, and in the air. Although more than 300 Tennessee clergymen became military chaplains during the course of the war, the supply never equaled the demand. Quotas were not met, even when educational and experience standards were lowered and age requirements were altered. Clerics who became chaplains were given full responsibility for the religious activities at their post as in their unit; this included counseling, visiting the sick and injured, officiating at baptisms, weddings, funerals, and conducting a general worship service. The nonsectarian character of the racially integrated Protestant worship services, which chaplains conducted and Tennessee soldiers and sailors attended, fostered a spirit of ecumenicity and dropped racial barriers, factors that were destined to alter social and religious life in the state when the war was over and the veterans returned home.

7. Conclusion

The nation had been at war for almost four years when the United States Air Force detonated two atomic bombs over Japan. The weapons — one dropped over Hiroshima on August 6, 1945, and the other over Nagasaki three days later — decreed the rapid end of World War II. The unprecedented devastation stunned the world and set off reverberations that were extremely difficult to comprehend or assess. But one thing was certain: the world would never be the same. A new era had suddenly emerged. Civilization's latest demonstration of the awesome potential of scientific knowledge had placed humanity at a dividing line and altered the seemingly orderly course of history. Was the new era — the "atomic age" — to be an age of atomic destruction? Or was it to be a new constructive era based on peaceful use of atomic energy?

The trauma of the two enormous blasts deepened for Americans when the road to destruction appeared the more imminent during the decade following Hiroshima and Nagasaki. As the "cold war" between the Communist Bloc and the Free World and the "hot war" that began in Korea in June 1950 created grave international tensions, anxious and insecure Americans feared that some overzealous Russian leader might, in a rash moment, trigger a series of events that would destroy mankind in a world holocaust. Yet the basic American inclination toward optimism was never fully abandoned.

The new era involved every major aspect of human affairs and American religious life was no exception. As frustrated, confused, desperate, but yet hopeful people looked to religion for reassurance, there was widespread feeling that its use of the bombs had placed the United States under obligation to provide moral leadership in the new age. So as denominations raised millions of dollars to send food and clothing to the war-torn countries of Europe, they also debated about the formation of the United Nations. Those who favored the project — mainly the liberal denominations — believed that the achievement of world peace depended greatly upon an effective international organization. But warning accompanied the endorsement: even with the United Nations, governments would have to subordinate their national interests to a higher moral law, and a large part of Tennessee church people were not about to agree to that.

Because of Communist commitment to atheism, a religious dimension was present in the confrontation between the Communist Bloc and the Free World. Many Americans, especially those in the more conservative denominations, viewed religion as a weapon to be employed in the struggle. In the helplessness and frustration of the time, being a church member or speaking favorably of religion was a means of affirming the "American way of life." Religious faith became an essential element in proper patriotic commitment. This popular resurgence of piety prompted the American Legion and the National Advertising Council to embark on "Back to God" and "Go to Church" campaigns. Soon the pledge of allegiance to the American flag was amended to include the phrase "under God," and the venerable statement "In God We Trust" became the country's official motto. Prayer breakfasts became daily occurrences and mass revivalism—also fed by an apocalypticism—came back into favor, with Billy Graham the best-known of the revivalists.

Tennessee shared the national spirit. After adopting resolutions giving thanks for the victorious end of war, several denominations in the state took official action in which they resolved to work for a better America and to "pray for new international relations which would be pleasing to God." Prayers for better relations abroad apparently brought reminders of unwholesome relationships at home; sincere efforts were immediately made to improve racial relations. Protesting "the injustice and indignities against blacks," the two largest bodies—Methodist and Southern Baptist—pledged to "conquor all prejudice" and to teach their children that "prejudice is unchristian."

Meanwhile, church attendance soared, membership increased, contributions mounted, and unprecedented sums were designated for new buildings, primarily in the suburban areas. Riding the crest of a wave of enthusiastic participation, religion had strong popular support.

The religious situation in Tennessee at the beginning of the "new age" was in sharp contrast with that of the age of settlement, almost 200 years earlier, when a few Christians gathered here and there to establish struggling congregations. Organized religion had come a long way! But more important, in the journey it had been a decidedly positive influence on Tennessee life. Congregations, with emphasis on a personal pietistic faith, had provided the moral and ethical leadership that transformed a rough and ready frontier into communities of law and order, and eventually into a stable society with tone. The educational institutions of the denominations, beacons of knowledge and virtue, singlehandedly, attacked the crudities of the backwoods and created a climate that produced successive generations of literate people that sought culture and refinement.

Selected Bibliography

Alexander, John. *The Synod of Tennessee.* Philadelphia: MacCalla, 1890.

Bailey, Kenneth. *Southern White Protestantism in the Twentieth Century.* New York: Harper, 1964.

Barrus, Ben; Milton Baughn; and Thomas Campbell. *A People Called Cumberland Presbyterians.* Memphis: Frontier Press, 1972.

Boles, John B. *Religion in Antebellum Kentucky.* Lexington: Univ. of Kentucky Press, 1976.

————. *The Great Revival: 1787–1805.* Lexington: Univ. of Kentucky Press, 1972.

Carter, Cullen. *History of the Tennessee Conference.* Nashville: Privately printed, 1948.

Coulter, E. Merton. *William G. Brownlow; Fighting Parson of the Southern Highlands.* Chapel Hill: Univ. of North Carolina Press, 1937; rpt. Knoxville: Univ. of Tennessee Press, 1971.

Davenport, F. Garvin. *Cultural Life in Nashville on the Eve of the Civil War.* Chapel Hill: Univ. of North Carolina Press, 1941.

Farish, Hunter. *The Circuit Rider Dismounts: A Social History of Southern Methodism, 1865–1900.* Richmond: Dietz Press, 1938.

Flanigan, George, ed. *Catholicity in Tennessee.* Nashville: Ambrose Printing Co., 1937.

Fuller, Thomas O. *History of the Negro Baptists of Tennessee.* Memphis: Privately printed, 1936.

Heishell, C.W. *Pioneer Presbyterians in Tennessee.* Richmond: Presbyterian Committee on Publications, 1898.

Hill, Samuel S., ed. *Religion and the Solid South.* Nashville: Abingdon Press, 1972.

Issac, Paul. *Prohibition and Politics: Turbulent Decades in Tennessee 1885–1920.* Knoxville: Univ. of Tennessee Press, 1965.

Johnson, Charles A. *The Frontier Camp Meeting.* Dallas: Southern Methodist Univ. Press, 1955.

Kendall, W. Fred. *A History of the Tennessee Baptist Convention.* Brentwood, Tenn.: Tennessee Baptist Convention, 1974.

Martin, Isaac. *History of Methodism in Holston Conference.* Knoxville: Methodist Historical Society of Holston Conference, 1945.

Morrow, Ralph. *Northern Methodism and Reconstruction.* East Lansing: Michigan State Univ. Press, 1956.

Norton, Herman. *Tennessee Christians.* Nashville: Reed and Co., 1971.

Posey, Walter B. *The Development of Methodism in the Old Southwest, 1783-1824.* Tuscaloosa: Weatherford Printing Co., 1933.

_____. *The Presbyterian Church in the Old Southwest, 1788-1838.* Richmond: John Knox Press, 1952.

_____. *The Baptist Church in the Lower Mississippi Valley, 1776-1845.* Lexington: Univ. of Kentucky Press, 1957.

_____. *Religious Strife on the Southern Frontier.* Baton Rouge: Louisiana State Univ. Press, 1965.

_____. *Frontier Mission: A History of Religion West of the Southern Appalachians to 1861.* Lexington: Univ. of Kentucky Press, 1966.

Seven Early Churches of Nashville. Nashville: Elder's Bookstore, 1972.

Spain, Rufus. *At Ease in Zion: Social History of the Southern Baptists, 1865-1900.* Nashville: Vanderbilt Univ. Press, 1961.

Taylor, Oury. *Early Tennessee Baptists, 1769-1832.* Nashville: Tennessee Baptist Convention, 1957.

Thompson, Ernest T. *Presbyterians in the South.* 3 vols. Richmond: John Knox Press, 1963-73.

Tucker, David. *Black Pastors and Leaders: Memphis 1819-1972.* Memphis: Memphis State Univ. Press, 1975.

Wallis, Charles, ed. *Autobiography of Peter Cartwright.* Nashville: Abingdon Press, 1956.

Index

Other Tennessee Three Star Books

Visions of Utopia
Nashoba, Rugby, Ruskin, and the "New Communities"
    in Tennessee's Past
by John Egerton

Our Restless Earth
The Geologic Regions of Tennessee
by Edward T. Luther

Tennessee Strings
The Story of Country Music in Tennessee
by Charles K. Wolfe

Paths of the Past
Tennessee, 1770–1970
by Paul H. Bergeron

Civil War Tennessee
Battles and Leaders
by Thomas L. Connelly

Tennessee's Indian Peoples
From White Contact to Removal, 1540–1840
by Ronald N. Satz

Tennessee's Presidents
by Frank B. Williams, Jr.

Blacks in Tennessee, 1791–1970
by Lester C. Lamon

Tennessee Writers
by Thomas Daniel Young

THE UNIVERSITY OF TENNESSEE PRESS : KNOXVILLE